Patricia P. Byrd

*"I have come to kindle
a fire on earth,
and how I wish
it were already burning"*
——Jesus*

*Luke 12:49, translation by J. Jeremias, *The Parables of Jesus,* p. 163.

STEP BY STEP
THROUGH THE PARABLES

*A beginner's guide to the modern
study of the stories Jesus told;
their meaning in his time and ours*

John W. Miller

PAULIST PRESS
New York/Ramsey

Acknowledgments

I would be remiss did I not acknowledge the contribution of Pauline Bauman to this book. Her meticulous care and patience in typing (and retyping!) always add a special touch of grace to the preparation of a manuscript of this nature. Also my students, more than I can begin to say, have been a stimulus in its evolution.

As with previous writing projects, my wife, Louise, has again been a steady source of helpful counsel and encouragement. Shortly after I completed the manuscript's initial draft, our first grandson, Scott Peace-Miller, was born. To him, as hopeful sign and joyful foretaste of yet another human generation, this book is gratefully dedicated, ". . . for to such belongs the kingdom of God" (Mark 10:14).

Unless stated otherwise, quotations of the Bible are from the Revised Standard Version; quotations of the Gospel of Thomas are from E. Hennecke, *New Testament Apocrypha,* edited by W. Schneemelcher (London: Lutterworth Press, 1963).

Library of Congress
Catalog Card Number: 81-80046

ISBN: 0-8091-2379-7

Published by Paulist Press
545 Island Road, Ramsey, N.J. 07446

Printed and bound in the
United States of America

CONTENTS

v

PART THREE
PARABLES EVOKING INSIGHT
INTO RIGHT AND WRONG WAYS
OF ACTING

for Scott,
three years old,
a delightful parable
of God's Kingdom

A Note to the Reader

This book is for the beginning student of Jesus' parables. My hope is that it might serve as a useful guide for individual or group study and lay a solid foundation for meaningful reflection on the message of these provocative stories both in their original setting and today.

The literature on the parables is already extensive. Why yet another book on this subject? Several abortive attempts at teaching the parables in lay settings persuaded me that most recent books on this subject (in spite of their excellence in other respects) are either too simple or too complex. Scholarly works tend to overwhelm the novice with too much data; popularizing studies often do not explain enough.

This is especially true, I have found, at the point of establishing the text of a given parable where there are differing versions. Scholarly works usually discuss these variant texts in great detail, the more popular studies hardly at all. Yet all present-day study of the parables is built on this foundation.

If there is anything unique about the book that follows, it may be the care with which I have tried to arrange the textual materials to be studied (and the steps to be followed in studying them). My hope is that with this manual in hand even the beginning student will be able to gain an understanding of the complex but highly important issues that sometimes confront us in this respect.

Opinions vary of course as to how much background information is needed before tackling a given text. Not every student will want to read through "Why and How Study the Parables" before actually studying them. Others may find the detailed textual work tedious. Every book of this kind requires adaptation to the needs of particular individuals and groups. A wise teacher is always of great help at this point.

I would urge those using this book as a manual for group study to note carefully the "Suggestions for Group Study" in the Appendix. The comments there are brief but imperative for a successful corporate study of this particular body of literature.

For additional resources the student should consult the annotated Bibliography. My notes there will also indicate something of the degree to which I have relied upon the labors of others. There are no footnotes in the following studies, but whenever a name is mentioned in the body of the discussion, additional information concerning the author's work and contribution can be found in the Bibliography.

I am confident that anyone putting forth the effort to engage in a study of Jesus' parables will be amply rewarded. These stories (with three or four exceptions) are not nearly as well known in the churches as they should be. As a result many Christians are missing a vital point of contact with the person they profess to revere above all others. Parables form the major block of Jesus' teachings. As such they represent a still unappropriated source of theological wisdom for the church in this last quarter of the twentieth century.

WHY AND HOW STUDY THE PARABLES?

A. WHY STUDY THE PARABLES?

According to Mark 4:34 Jesus rarely or never taught "without a parable." It was the most striking characteristic of his teaching style. This is confirmed by the proportionately large number of parables in the Gospels. About a third of all the teachings of Jesus recorded there are "in parables."

For Christians this should be reason enough for giving high priority to the study of these stories. Reverence for Jesus as teacher is at the core of Christianity, and his parables convey his unique way of looking at life.

In the parables we come as close as we can hope to come to "the mind of Christ." This being so, it may seem odd (at first glance) that the parables of Jesus are so seldom studied and often poorly understood. It is the rare Christian, I have found, who can name a fourth of them or retell any of them, and this in spite of years of Sunday school and church attendance.

There is a reason, however, for this state of affairs. The form of the parable, for one thing, is a mystery to most of us. In modern discourse we do not often use parables, at least not parables of the kind Jesus told. We also lack precise information, in many instances, as to when, where or with reference to what issue these stories were first spoken. They are like sermon illustrations without the sermon. As

1

a result their original point frequently eludes us. Small wonder that lay groups avoid these stories, or when they do study them, often bog down in a quagmire of subjective and conflicting points of view.

Before launching a study of Jesus' parables it is imperative that attention be paid to procedure. *In parables-study especially, failure to establish proper study methods will prove fatal to the whole enterprise.*

B. HOW STUDY THE PARABLES?

Three questions are important for determining how the parables should be studied. First, what is a parable? Second, how does a parable work? And third, how has it come about that we have differing versions of the same parable?

(1) What is a parable?

It goes without saying that the nature of an object determines how we go about studying it. We don't study a microbe the way we study a literary document. And we don't study a calculus textbook the way we study a poem. Crucial to the study of the parables is awareness of what a parable is.

In defining what we mean by "parable" it should be emphasized that the term is of interest to us here only as it relates to some forty stories that Jesus told. Our focus is not on the word "parable" as literary classification in itself, but on beginning to understand the parables of Jesus. Careful study of each parable will reveal its unique qualities. In doing this we will discover that not all of these stories neatly conform to a single definition.

It is apparent, however, that the larger number of them do exhibit certain common characteristics, and for this reason are referred to in the Gospels as "parables." What is meant by this term?

"Parable" is a Greek word combining the prefix "*para-*" ("beside") with the verb "*ballain*" ("to throw"). In a parable dissimilar yet similar things are "thrown" or put side by side. In short, a parable is a comparison.

Saying this much, however, is only an explanatory first step.

Comparisons in general are the stock in trade of every teacher, since it is by comparing one thing to another that learning mostly takes place. But comparisons can take many forms. What, more precisely, is the unique form of those comparisons we call the parables of Jesus?

Before answering this question we should consider a few alternatives in the art of comparing. One of the more important distinctions in this respect is between comparisons that are explicit and those that are vague. "All we like sheep have gone astray," is a familiar example of an explicit comparison. "We" are compared to "sheep" in their tendency to go astray. The word "like" makes unmistakably clear the connection between the two. Comparisons of this type are called similes.

But if someone were to say, "There are certainly a lot of sheep going astray these days," this too, conceivably, might be a comparison. At first, however, we are puzzled. It is not stated in so many words that by "sheep" is meant something else. Nor are we told to whom or to what the comparison (if it is one) refers. But context and manner may suggest that the speaker does in fact refer, not to sheep, but to people. Suddenly we are struck by the thought that many of *us* "are going astray these days." This more subtle mode of comparing is called a metaphor.

Another distinction can be drawn between longer and shorter comparisons. Taking the picture of the straying sheep, we might expand it into a story about a shepherd who lost one of his sheep. We might go on to tell how the shepherd went looking for it until he found it, and then rejoiced with his friends over his good fortune. Here the comparison is housed not in a single sentence but in the dynamic of a story. Obviously this brings us close to what is meant by the term "parable" in the Gospels.

The parables of Jesus are comparisons, generally subtle rather than explicit and longer rather than shorter. They might be called metaphorical stories.

(2) How do the parables work?

It is not enough, however, to describe a parable in terms of its literary form. Even more important is to gain some appreciation for the way it functions. What kind of an effect were the parables of Jesus intended to have on their audiences? Why did Jesus speak in parables? Four observations may help us in answering these questions.

(a) First of all, it is important to recall that Jesus did in fact "speak" in parables. Before these stories were written down they were told. Whatever meaning they were meant to convey was conveyed by way of the voice and the ear. One "caught" their meaning by listening and thinking, rather than by reading and study. The dynamic of the story thus had to be relatively simple and direct. Its telling must have been vigorous, its impact dramatic. This observation has important implications for the way we should study the parables today. More will be said about this later on.

(b) Through his parables Jesus sought to confront and enlighten specific audiences. Like the prophet Nathan before King David in the wake of his sin with Bathsheba (II Sam. 12) *Jesus used parables to communicate passionately felt truth in concrete settings.*

This is only what we might expect and would hardly merit further discussion were it not that Mark 4:10ff. seems to describe the function of the parables somewhat differently. There we read that after Jesus had taught a very large crowd beside the sea, using parables, he withdrew. "And when he was alone [the narrative continues], those who were about him with the twelve asked him concerning the parables."

Jesus answered:

> To you has been given the secret of the kingdom of God, but for those outside everything is in parables; *so that* they may indeed see but not perceive, and may indeed hear but not understand; *lest* they should turn again, and be forgiven.

It is certainly difficult to read this passage and imagine that Jesus had "confrontation" and "enlightenment" in mind when he first used these stories. It is implied rather that parables were told to *hide* the "secret" of the kingdom from those "outside," "so that they may indeed see but not perceive . . ." But even those "inside" the intimate circle of disciples are described (in the following verses) as being perplexed by the parables. They do not understand, for example, what

Jesus meant by his parable of the Sower (Mark 4:13). Jesus must therefore explain it to them (Mark 4:14–20).

After reading the explanation given, one can see why. The parable of the Sower, we are told, is packed full of symbolism. The "seed," for example, is said to be symbolic of the "word"; the birds that snatch it away represent "Satan"; the soils into which the seed falls are people in their differing responses to the word; the sun beating down on the seed refers to persecution; the thorns are worldly cares and desires. The parable of the Sower, in short, is interpreted as though it were a full-blown allegory.

A parable, we suggested above, is a fairly simple, metaphorical story. It was spoken, and its audience "caught" its meaning through listening to the dynamic of the tale as a whole. An allegory, on the other hand, is more complex. It must be studied. Its meaning lies not in its overall thrust, but in its various details, each of which has a veiled symbolic reference to something else. To understand an allegory, more often than not, one needs an interpretative "key." To those "outside" its meaning is "hidden."

Mark 4:10ff. suggests that all the parables should be read as though they were allegories. The crowds to which they were initially spoken could not understand them. Indeed, it is said, they were not supposed to understand them," *lest* they should turn again and be forgiven." Only an inner circle of disciples is privileged to know their real meaning through special teaching that explains the allegorical code.

Partly because of Mark 4:10–12 (and the accompanying allegory) this way of looking at the parables has dominated parable study until recent times. It still prevails in many popular expositions. A frequently cited example of how earlier scriptural scholars made use of this method is Augustine's allegorical interpretation of the parable of the Good Samaritan. On the surface this parable would appear to be a rather straightforward story. But no, Augustine wrote, this parable too, like the story of the Sower, contains a multiplicity of hidden meanings, if only the reader has ears to hear. The man who went down from Jerusalem to Jericho is a symbol of Adam, Augustine wrote. The fact that he "went *down* from Jerusalem" refers to the fall of Adam from blessedness. The thieves who stripped him are the devil and his angels. When it says they stripped him, it means they took away his immortality and "beat" him into sin. They left him "half dead," suggesting the present condition of mankind, half alive toward God and half dead in sin. And so Augustine proceeded, point by point, through the entire parable, attaching significance to virtually every detail. The Samaritan is Jesus, the inn is the church, and the innkeeper is the Apostle Paul!

It is one of the major achievements of recent study of the Gospels to have successfully challenged this imaginative but arbitrary way of interpreting Jesus' parables. Mark 4:10–12, it is now recognized, reflects more the thought-world of early Christianity than that of Jesus (see below for further comments on the formation of the Gospel traditions). In fact, the idea expressed here that Jesus taught so that the Jewish masses would *not* understand (lest they turn and be forgiven) is very similar to Paul's daring insight that it was God's *intention* that a "hardening" came upon a part of Israel, "until the full number of the Gentiles has come in" (Rom. 11:25, 9:18–29, 10:16–21, 11:7–11). Mark 4:10–12 differs from this only in intimating that *Jesus himself* fostered this "hardening" through his oblique, impossible-to-understand allegorical method of teaching (Carlston). As we shall see, this picture of Jesus' purpose in telling his parables is contradicted by a closer study of virtually every story dealt with in the following pages. *A sharp focus on Jesus' parables in their most original form and setting will reveal again and again that their purpose was not to mystify but to communicate, not to hide the truth but to release it, and in very concrete, specific situations.*

But how does a parable do this? If intended for enlightenment, how does it actually work?

(c) Parables stir the imagination and stimulate personal involvement and search. The parable invites its audience to live, for a few moments, in another world. In this respect it is similar to a drama or play. The audience of a parable is not permitted to remain passive. It must project itself into the "metaphorical story" if it wishes to understand it. It must live with the farmer as he sows his field. It must share in the petty frustrations of children fighting at their games. It must go with the wayward son as he travels into a far country. It must watch the woman as she prepares the dough for the baking of bread.

And as the audience does so, it is compelled to search. What is the teller of this parable really trying to say? At first one does not quite know. The mind probes this way and that. If the search is pursued and not too easily given up, a light begins to shine. Insight dawns. One may well have what psychologists call an "Aha" experience.

"At its simplest," writes C. H. Dodd in his justly famous book on the parables *(The Parables of the Kingdom),* "the parable is a metaphor or simile drawn from nature or common life, arresting the hearer by its vividness or strangeness, and leaving the mind in sufficient doubt about its precise application to tease it into active thought."

A parable does not so much convey a finished truth as it precipitates an experience and opens up into a highly personal search.

All this is graphically illustrated by the account in Luke 7:36–50 of Jesus' visit to the home of a Pharisee. There we are told that Jesus confronted the icy hostility that enveloped him, when a "sinner" anointed his feet, by telling a parable. The parable formulated for this occasion was a simple one that spoke of two men in debt, but disproportionately so. One owed 500 denarii, the other only 50. Both debtors were forgiven. "Now which of them will have the greater love for the one who forgave them?" Jesus inquired of his host.

Simon the Pharisee is not directly challenged. He is invited instead to use his imagination. The parables spring from the conviction that those who are enticed to seek shall find and that those who knock will have a door opened to them. Their function is precisely to awaken this searching and knocking at the door of truth.

(d) The parables keep on working as parables. Sometimes the parables have been viewed as "containers," carrying a truth that can exist just as well apart from the parable. Viewed in this way, the parable becomes expendable at the point where the truth or maxim being "carried" is "delivered."

Contemporary students of the parables, however, are beginning to see a metaphorical story somewhat differently. Authentic metaphors are very rare creatures, we are beginning to realize, and say something that cannot be said as well in any other way. The truth they convey, writes John Crossan, "cannot rise above the truth of the original metaphor." If this is true, the only way of gaining access to the message of Jesus in his parables is by retelling and reliving them. I will have more to say about this point later on when identifying the steps to be taken in parable study (see the discussion of step five).

(3) Why differing versions of the same parable?

Having said something about what a parable is and how it functions, it might seem we should now be ready to establish proper study procedures.

Before doing that, however, there is an additional matter that merits serious consideration: The puzzling fact that in many instances the Gospels record differing versions of the same parable.

A glance at the table of contents of this book will indicate the extent of these multiple versions. The textual differences between them are numerous and sometimes significant.

Most lay-oriented study guides to the parables pay as little attention to these textual problems as possible. More serious studies examine them in great detail. Analysis of these textual differences has contributed significantly to the breakthrough in parables study (away from allegory) referred to above. *Careful textual work is the indispensable key to the understanding of the parables in their earliest form and meaning.*

For this and other reasons I consider it imperative that lay study groups also become acquainted with this exciting phase of parable study. While, to be sure, there are technical problems at this point that only those familiar with the original languages of the Bible can fully understand, in most instances the observations required are of a kind that any intelligent person can make, given a proper arrangement of the texts in parallel columns (see Burton Throckmorton, Jr., *Gospel Parallels*).

In this manual, then, I have chosen not to avoid these textual variations. *Observing and interpreting the differences that occur between parallel versions of the same parable is a vital part of the study process.* Something therefore must be said by way of orientation to this subject.

A concrete example of what we are talking about will help to focus the problem at hand. The already mentioned parable of the

Lost Sheep can serve this purpose, for it appears twice in the Gospel records, once in Matthew 18:12–14 and again in Luke 15:3–7. Even a quick glance at these two texts will reveal that they are somewhat different. This immediately confronts us with a decision: in trying to understand this parable, which text shall we study? In order to make that decision, we must of course note more precisely what the differences between the two texts actually are and what their significance might be. This requires that we print the two texts side by side and compare them (before proceeding, the reader should do this, underscoring the words in Luke's text that differ or do not appear in Matthew):

Matthew 18:12–14	Luke 15:3–7
What do you think? If a man has a hundred sheep, and one of them has gone astray, does he not leave the ninety-nine on the hills and go in search of the one that went astray? And if he finds it, truly, I say to you, he rejoices over it more than over the ninety-nine that never went astray.	What man of you, having a hundred sheep, if he has lost one of them, does not leave the ninety-nine in the wilderness, and go after the one which is lost, until he finds it? And when he has found it, he lays it on his shoulders, rejoicing. And when he comes home, he calls together his friends and his neighbors, saying to them, "Rejoice with me, for I have found my sheep which was lost."
So it is not the will of my Father who is in heaven that one of these little ones should perish.	Just so, I tell you, there will be more joy in heaven over one sinner who repents than over ninety-nine righteous persons who need no repentance.

It will be noted first of all that the two texts are strikingly similar. Subject matter and plot are identical, leaving little doubt that the texts in Matthew and Luke are indeed versions of the same parable.

But equally obvious is the fact that Luke's version is longer. Missing from Matthew's text is the scene where the shepherd returns home after finding the sheep and summons his friends to a party. But this is by no means the only difference. Reading the two stories still more carefully, we become aware of several minor variations in vocabulary and phrasing. In Luke for example, the sheep is described as "lost"; in Matthew it "went astray." In Luke the shepherd goes seeking the sheep "until he finds it." When he finds it he "lays it on his shoulder." Both phrases are missing in Matthew. The parable is formulated as a question in Luke ("What man . . ."); it is prefaced by a question in Matthew ("What do you think?"). Luke's parable comes to its close with a comment about "joy in heaven" over the sinner who repents. Matthew's version closes with a statement concerning the Father's will that none of "these little ones" shall perish.

In addition to the differences in the parable itself, a glance at the *context* of the story in each Gospel reveals another set of dissimilarities. In Matthew the parable is set within the framework of a larger collection of sayings all having to do with the theme of mutual responsibility of "disciples" (18:1) within the setting of the "church" (Matt. 18:17). Luke, on the other hand, locates the parable in the context of Jesus' debate with the Pharisees over what attitude should be taken toward ostracized Jewish "sinners" (Luke 15:1f.).

Here is only one example among many of the striking differences that can be observed in multiple versions of the same parable. How are we to explain textual and contextual variations such as these?

To begin answering this question *it is important that we try to visualize something of the process of transmission through which Jesus' teachings must have gone prior to their inclusion in the Gospels as we now have them.* Although a great deal of study has been devoted to this matter, the results are still relatively unknown to the great majority of Christians.

It must be remembered, first of all, that Jesus himself did no writing. His entire teaching activity, like that of his Rabbinic contemporaries, was carried on exclusively by means of *oral* communication.

The question that poses itself then is this: *How did it come about that teachings which were at first oral and unwritten were nevertheless preserved and eventually recorded in the Gospels?* In arriving at an answer to this important question modern scholars have identified three moments in particular as critical to this transmission process: The moment when the teachings were first given in the lifetime of Jesus; the time of their use as instruction in the early Christian churches; and their collection and editing by the authors of the Gos-

pels. A few comments about each of these stages of transmission may
be in order at this point.

(a) The first critical moment in the transmission of Jesus' words
occurred of course when Jesus initially spoke them (in Aramaic, his
mother tongue). Studies related to this phase of the process are often
referred to as "historical Jesus" studies. As we try to imagine the circumstances of this original teaching activity, one thing above all
must be kept in mind: Jesus was rather constantly accompanied, during this time of life, by chosen disciples. According to the customs
of that age, it was a primary responsibility of disciples to memorize
the teachings of their master. Thus while it is true that Jesus' teachings were originally oral and unwritten, they were not unrecorded.
Rather they were carefully preserved in the memory of his disciples.

What then did these first disciples do with the teachings?

(b) Of one thing we can be certain: they shared what they had
received from Jesus with that growing circle of persons who began
joining the Christian movement after Jesus' death and resurrection.
The words of Jesus, spoken initially in Aramaic to Jewish audiences
in Palestine, prior to his crucifixion, were now gradually translated
into Greek and put to use as instruction for those who were "being
added daily to their number" (Acts 2:47). Study focusing on the
ways in which the original teachings were shaped by use in the Palestinian and Greek-speaking churches is sometimes called "form-
criticism."

At this point too the teaching was mainly done by means of oral
communication. We don't know when these teachings were first
written down. Luke indicates in the preface to his Gospel that by his
time in any case (some forty years after Jesus' death) there were
those who had begun "to draw up accounts" (Luke 1:1). *The point
to be stressed, however, about this second stage in the transmission
process is that during this time (from about A.D. 30 to 70) the words
and parables of Jesus were circulating among the Christian churches
and being used there for instruction in Christian living.*

(c) A third moment, or stage, in the transmission of the parables arrived when these teachings in oral and written form were
gathered up into those larger accounts of the life of Jesus we call
Gospels. To understand fully how this happened would require far
more space and time than can possibly be devoted to the question

here. We will have to confine ourselves to those observations that are of prime importance for interpreting the parables and for explaining the variations between parallel texts.

This means, first of all, that we can limit our discussion at this point to Matthew, Mark and Luke, since none of the thirty-six parables studied in this manual appears in John's Gospel. This is only one of many features of the Johannine Gospel that set it apart from the so-called "synoptic" Gospels (Matthew, Mark and Luke).

Our question then is this: *How did Matthew, Mark and Luke come to be written? And why do they so frequently record the same parables, but in differing versions and in different contexts?*

Many lay people, I discover, still think of the composition of these Gospels as though they were biographies written largely from memory. They imagine the Gospel authors sitting down at a desk, pen in hand, and rather freely composing their accounts of Jesus' life and words, without any help except their own personal recollections of what happened.

But this picture begins to break down as soon as we read what Luke, for example, wrote about his Gospel in its preface (Luke 1:1–4). Luke of course was not among the original disciples of Jesus. There was no possibility, then, of his writing about Jesus from memory. He had to rely on the testimony of others for the "orderly account" he wished to put together. He specifically informs us that "many" before him had already begun to compile records of "the things which have been accomplished among us." No doubt he examined these accounts and made use of them.

The Gospel of Luke is not then a free composition. It was, in part at least, "compiled" from a variety of oral and written sources.

Although we do not have similar prefaces describing how the Gospels of Matthew and Mark were composed, careful study has demonstrated that a similar method must have been followed in these Gospels as well.

Consider, for example, the following well-known facts: Mark has 661 verses. All but 55 of these verses are also found (in one form or another) in Matthew. About half of them (320) also appear in Luke. Only 31 of Mark's 661 verses do not reappear in either Matthew or Luke. In other words, virtually all of Mark is found as well in Matthew and Luke. How is this rather massive duplication of materials to be explained? It would appear that the Gospel writers borrowed from each other or from a common source. But who was borrowing from whom? (On all this, see William Barclay, *The Gospels & Acts.*)

After studying the matter carefully, the majority of scholars have concluded that Matthew and Luke were for the most part borrowing from Mark. In composing their Gospels they may well have had a version of Mark's Gospel before them. If this was the case, it is apparent through comparing the same texts in the three Gospels that they did not hesitate adapting the material they borrowed. At many points they introduced both a different arrangement and a modification of wording. Matthew, for example, rather consistently shortens the borrowed material, apparently to make room for his enlarged collection of teachings.

Matthew and Luke of course did not confine their editorial borrowings to Mark. Scholars believe, for example, that they also used a prior collection of Jesus' "sayings" (the so-called "Q" source). From this they obtained the some 250 verses that are common to their Gospels but that do not appear in Mark. Matthew and Luke must also have had access to oral traditions about Jesus circulating in the churches of which they were members.

Perhaps enough has been said, however, to make the point that the Gospels in which the parables appear are, for the most part, based on older sources. *The third major step in the transmission of Jesus' words occurred when the oral and written traditions about Jesus, circulating in the churches, were collected and edited by the authors of the synoptic Gospels.*

Study of the way the Gospel authors went about doing this is sometimes called "redaction (or editorial) criticism."

Now what is the significance of all this for the task at hand? How does knowledge of this process by which the teachings of Jesus were preserved explain the fact that we have differing versions of the same parable?

It might be well to recapitulate the main points just made. The parables, we suggested, were first told by Jesus to audiences of Jews in Palestine. This is their original historical setting. They were remembered by Jesus' disciples and retold within the Christian churches for instruction in Christian living. This is their second setting. Finally they were brought together in the framework of larger Gospels.

The differences that occur between versions of the same parable can best be explained in the light of these differing "moments" in transmission. Some versions of the parables are closer than others to the form of the story originally told by Jesus. Others represent the way the parable was adapted for use in the early Christian churches. Still other versions may be the result of editorial work on the part of the Gospel authors.

The parable of the Lost Sheep can again serve as an example. Luke and Matthew, as noted, each locate this parable in a quite different context in their Gospels. Luke's setting indicates that he understood the parable as relating to a very specific issue in the life of Jesus: his controversy with the Pharisees over their attitude toward Jewish "sinners." The wording of the parable is consistent with this point of view. *Luke, in other words, has preserved the story in the setting of Jesus' life.*

Matthew's version of the parable reflects its adaptation for use in the early Christian churches. There it was seen as speaking to the question of what attitude Christian leaders should take toward "straying little ones" (the term Matthew used for church members). The central thrust of the parable is similar in both instances, but it has been changed somewhat by Matthew, or his church, to answer to a new issue.

(4) Which texts shall we study?

As can be seen from the example just given, and as we shall discover in many other instances, parallel versions of the same parable (especially where the variations between them are significant) confront us with a choice: Which version of a given parable shall we study?

Recently in fact the range of choices was enlarged by the translation and publication of the Gospel according to Thomas. This Gospel is one of thirteen manuscripts discovered in 1945 in a Gnostic library in Upper Egypt (Nag-Hamadi). It is not really a Gospel in the canonical sense, since it tells us virtually nothing about the life of Jesus. It is rather a collection of 114 "secret words" purportedly spoken to the disciple Didymos Judas Thomas by the "living Jesus." Many of these 114 teachings are rather strange and hard to imagine on the lips of the Jesus of history. Others, however, directly parallel the teachings of Jesus in the Gospels. Among these are twelve parables, some of which differ at points from the synoptic versions. (See Ray Summers, *The Secret Sayings of the Living Jesus.*)

So the question is: Which of the various texts available shall be the object of our study?

It goes without saying that all of them are worth studying. Some texts, however, as previously noted reflect the meaning the parables came to have for Christians in the early church. *In this manual our focus will be centered on the meaning the parables had when Jesus first told them. As a consequence we will study those texts that are nearest to the form they might have had in the setting of his life.*

This focus is dictated partly by limitations of space and time. To study the meaning the parables had for the early Christians (as well as for Jesus and his contemporaries) would require a book twice the size of the present one. *It also reflects the widespread conviction among students of the parables that the only way to control the interpretation of these stories in the church, and save them from meaning whatever anyone wants them to mean, is by discovering what they were intended to communicate when first told.* Needless to say, in focusing on the original meaning of the stories we are also expressing our desire to know more about that one who is the recognized fountainhead of the Christian tradition and its most respected teacher and Lord.

(5) Characteristics of the earliest versions

If our goal, then, is to study the earliest versions of the parables, how (in cases where differing versions are available) can we identify these? What are the characteristics of a story told by Jesus? How does it differ from the way the stories were often retold by the early Christians?

The answer to these questions must be arrived at by patient study of each parable in question. But some preliminary idea of what others have discovered might be useful to the beginning student as a guide through what may appear at first to be a maze of confusing and unexplainable textual variations.

(a) The earliest versions of Jesus' parables are usually but not always the shortest ones. In retelling a story that was short to begin with, there is a tendency to embellish it. It may also happen, however, that important features of the story are dropped out. Matthew in particular sometimes shortens the texts he borrows from his sources in order to conserve space. So this is not always a reliable guide in and of itself.

(b) A more discriminating characteristic of the earliest versions is their naturalness and inner consistency. The parables of Jesus, as he told them, tell of things that "might have actually happened." Their plots are simple and true to life. Where there are two or more versions and one of them has this characteristic, and the other does not, the original parable is the simpler and more natural one.

(c) Closely related is the freedom from allegorical embellishments in the earlier versions. Allegorical over-interpretations of Jesus stories became popular among the early Christians and remain so to the present time (see our previous discussion of this point above). This reflects a later and mostly literary stage in the study of the parables. Originally Jesus' parables were simple stories whose meaning was apparent to those who had "ears to hear." Where expansions in an allegorical direction are in evidence, this is almost always a sign of a later version.

(d) The earliest versions were also, for the most part, free of moralizing or sermonizing additions. Their original intent was to evoke rather than to explain, elicit a train of thought rather than to sermonize. Where short epigrams or sayings are appended to a parable, closer study will demonstrate that in many instances these were added by the church or the Gospel editors, and were not a feature of the original stories.

(e) Finally, the earliest versions "fit" to one or another of the well-known issues or themes in the life of Jesus. They reflect his milieu and his language. In short, they "feel" more consistent with all that we know from other sources about Jesus' life and times. The later versions, on the other hand, reflect the language, life and times of the early church.

(b) Steps in parable study

The discussion to this point will no doubt have made at least this much clear: the study of Jesus' parables is fraught with difficulties! But it has also, I hope, begun to point the way through these difficulties. It is time that we turn to a study of the parables themselves. Before doing so let us try to summarize the significance of our discussion thus far for the work that lies ahead.

Knowledge of what the parables of Jesus are and how they function, as well as awareness of how it has happened that there are differing versions of the same parable, leads to the following study suggestions. I list them as steps, in order to indicate the importance of pursuing them in rather strict sequence (as indeed we will be doing in the following studies):

(a) *Step One: Getting oriented.* If our goal is to understand the parables in the setting in which they were *originally* told, we cannot assume that their present context in the Gospels will help us at this point. As previously noted, by the time the Gospels were written, information about when, where, and why Jesus told specific parables was no longer accessible. Also the Gospel editors, as they arranged the teachings available to them, had other than historical concerns in mind. *Step One in parables study is to become aware of this fact and to ask, in a provisional way, about the setting or theme in Jesus' ministry to which a given parable might belong.* In "getting oriented" we begin to feel our way toward the possible meaning of the parables in the lifetime of Jesus.

(b) *Step Two: Getting acquainted with the text or texts.* Here, of course, is where the study really begins. Careful observation of the text of the parables is the indispensable foundation of all that follows. Where several texts of a specific parable exist, each one must be studied and compared with the others. Memorizing and telling the parables can be very useful at this point in beginning to grasp their inner dynamic (see our suggestions for group study in the Appendix). It must always be borne in mind that these stories were first spoken and heard, not written and read.

(c) *Step Three: Deciding which text to study.* Where more than one text exists and they differ markedly from each other, a decision will need to be made about which text to concentrate on for further study. As suggested above, all the texts are worthy of study, but our interest in this manual focuses on the earlier rather than the later versions, on the form of the parable as taught by Jesus, rather than the form it took in the early church. At Step Three in the study process it is well to summarize the reasons for choosing one text over another as more representative of its earliest available form.

(d) *Step Four: Meaning in the setting of Jesus' life.* A common danger in lay study of the parables is to move too quickly from the text of a parable to its relevance for today without considering its original meaning. When we do this the parable loses its power to speak *to* us, and is reduced to a device for saying what *we* want to say. To avoid this recycling of our own thoughts we must first discover what *Jesus* wanted to say through the parables in the setting of *his* lifetime. At this point in our study we can correct, fill out, or abandon (as the case may be) the suggestions tentatively put forward in Step One.

(e) *Step Five: Listening to the parable today.* We can now explore the present meaning of the parables. Obviously parables study is not for those who want quick results with a minimum of effort. But if we patiently live with these stories they will grow luminous with meaning. At this point, if not before, the parable under discussion should be memorized so that it can be told and retold easily. It is not enough to identify a parable's meaning, retain that, and then put the story aside. No, the story itself should be stored up in our memories. Then *as a parable* it will keep on working in our consciousness reminding us of things past and present. During this step, as much time as necessary should be taken to identify the thoughts that were awakened during the entire study process (see again suggestions for group study in the Appendix).

(7) How many parables are there?

A further comment or two might yet be in order in explanation of the number of stories selected for study in this book. A glance at the literature on the parables will reveal a certain amount of variation as to which of Jesus' teachings to classify as parables. The range fluctuates between thirty and sixty and depends largely on how

many of Jesus' shorter figurative sayings are included in this catego-
ry. I have been somewhat conservative at this point, treating as parables only those metaphors that are definitely expanded into
something like a story. Even of this group, several parables have been
bypassed in this manual either because their text is especially uncertain, or because of widespread unclarity as to their meaning. Among
those avoided for these reasons are the parables of the Seine-net
(Matt. 13:47f.), the Closed Door (Luke 13:24–30), the Burglar (Matt.
24:43f./Luke 12:39f./Thomas 21b), and the Doorkeeper (Mark
13:33–37/Luke 12:35–38). The thirty-six parables discussed are the
hard core of the tradition.

PART ONE

PARABLES EXPRESSING CONFIDENCE IN GOD AND THE COMING OF GOD'S KINGDOM

You shall love the Lord with all your heart, and with all your soul, and with all your mind, and with all your strength (Mark 12:30/Luke 10:27/ Matt. 22:37).

I. CONFIDENCE IN GOD

1. THE WICKED JUDGE (Luke 18:1–8)

(a) Getting oriented

In what order shall we study the parables? Any answer we give will be somewhat arbitrary. The Gospel editors themselves follow differing approaches. Most often they group the parables according to themes; at other times they seem to be guided by their intuition as to the place of a given parable in the setting of Jesus' life.

A glance at the table of contents will indicate that I have chosen in the following studies to arrange the parables thematically. But around what themes do the parables most naturally group themselves?

It is well known how Jesus cited the commandments to love God *and* neighbor as the greatest of all spiritual laws (Mark 12:30/Luke 10:27/Matt. 22:37). I have been impressed as I have studied the parables by their relationship to this dual emphasis. About half of Jesus' parables can be readily grouped around the theme of love for God (Part One of our study) and love for neighbor (Part Two of our study). The other half explore the various ways people respond or avoid responding to this challenge (Part Three of the following study).

This way of grouping the parables may also reflect, broadly speaking, the chronological shape of Jesus' public career. There are reasons for believing that the central theme of the *opening* phase of Jesus' Galilean mission was "good news of God" (Mark 1:14) for the "poor," the "sinner," the disaffiliated (Mark 2:17; Matt. 11:5/Luke 7:22). This corresponds to the parables we have grouped around the topic "Confidence in God and the coming of God's kingdom" in this opening section of our study.

However, this first phase of Jesus' mission was interrupted by searing criticism. Jesus' friendly association with "sinners" (Matt. 11:19/Luke 7:34) became the target of suspicions on the part of the Pharisaic leaders of the Jewish synagogue (Luke 15:1f.). As a consequence he was compelled to defend himself, and did so by telling a cluster of unforgettable stories advocating forgiveness, compassion, humility ("love for neighbor," Part Two of our study).

As this fateful dialogue with the Jewish establishment progressed, the conviction grew that in the repentance movement among the disaffiliated, spearheaded by John the Baptist and himself (Luke 7:24–35; Matt. 21:28–32; Mark 11:27–33), Judaism was faced with a challenge of fateful consequences. A hardening seemed to be settling over the Jewish elite. A too self-righteous attitude threatened to fragment the Jewish people internally and foster an alarming hostility toward Rome. Unchecked, these tendencies might well lead to catastrophe (Luke 13:1–5; 19:41–44). A progressively intense confrontation on Jesus' part with the representatives of this attitude is reflected in the parables of Part Three.

From this brief survey of the possible settings in the life of Jesus of the parables we will be studying it is already apparent that their original audiences were diverse. Most of the parables in this first section were no doubt spoken to those who were open and responsive to Jesus' hopeful message about God. The great majority of the remaining parables (Parts Two and Three) may have been addressed to Jesus' critics.

The first commandment, said Jesus, is to love God. The "Gospel of God" was also, as just noted, the central theme of the opening phase of his mission. With this in mind we will turn initially to those parables that speak metaphorically of God and God's kingdom.

Among these are two stories that approach this topic in an especially provocative way. One of them is traditionally known as the parable of the Unjust (or Wicked) Judge.

(b) Getting acquainted with the text

Only Luke records the text of this parable, but few have doubted that it is very much as Jesus must have told it. It is important, however, to observe where the parable itself actually begins and ends. In this instance the parable is prefaced by an *editorial introduction,* possibly from the hand of Luke: "And he told them a parable, to the effect that they ought always to pray and not lose heart. He said . . ." Also appended to the parable is an explanatory statement ascribed to "the Lord."

> And the Lord said, "Hear what the unrighteous judge says. And will not God vindicate his elect, who cry to him day and night? Will he delay long over them? I tell you, he will vindicate them speedily. Nevertheless, when the Son of man comes, will he find faith on earth?"

A comparison of these opening and closing comments reveals that they do not completely agree as to the parable's meaning. Luke's preface would suggest that this parable is primarily about a *widow* and her persistence (always pray like this widow and do not lose heart). But the appended comments from the "Lord" invite us to listen to the *judge* ("Hear what the unrighteous judge says").

Is the widow or the judge the key figure? To answer we must turn to the parable itself and listen to what it has to say in its own right.

> In a certain city there was a judge who neither feared God nor regarded man; and there was a widow in that city who kept coming to him and saying, "Vindicate me against my adversary."
>
> For a while he refused; but afterward he said to himself, "Though I neither fear God nor regard man, yet because this widow bothers me, I will vindicate her, or she will wear me out by her continual coming."

Note that the parable itself begins by riveting our attention on the judge ("In a certain city there was a *judge* . . ."). And again it is the judge who is center stage in the parable's final, climactic scene. There this wicked fellow mumbles to himself (rather humorously) that even though it is true that he has no regard for God or man, he'll be worn out if this widow keeps on pestering him much longer. So he'll just have to compromise himself and do something good for a change! The widow's role in this story simply highlights the fact that even a thoroughly despicable judge will do a good deed once in a while, even if for not very good reasons.

(c) Deciding which text to study

Bear in mind that Luke's editorial preface is an example of early Christian interpretation, not necessarily what the parable *originally* meant. The appended comments attributed to the "Lord" might indeed go back to Jesus himself. If so, they are an important clue to interpretation. But in any case, the parable itself should be studied apart from the comments that surround it.

(d) Meaning in the setting of Jesus' life

Both the parable and the appended comments focus our attention on the wicked judge and suggest that Jesus told this parable originally to awaken faith. If even a bad judge will respond to the cries of a poor widow, "will not *God* vindicate those who cry to *him* . . . I tell you *he will* . . ."

This parable is not then, first of all, about prayer (as Luke's preface implies), but about the trustworthiness of God. That of course has implications for prayer. But it would be a mistake to center too much attention on the widow's desperate persistence and take that as the parable's central meaning. Rather, Jesus' eye was on the judge, whose humorously self-serving but helpful action points to the infinitely greater goodness of God.

This parable is a window into the mind of Jesus. It shows us how deeply he believed that God is good (Mark 10:18; Matt. 5:43–48), and that those who turn to God will find a gracious reception and response (Matt. 6:5–8).

Before opening ourselves to the relevance of this parable for today, let's turn to another story with a similar thrust.

2. GOING TO A FRIEND AT MIDNIGHT
(Luke 11:5–8)

(a) Getting oriented

Having decided to begin our study of the parables with the story of the Wicked Judge, there is little question as to which parable we should study next. "Going to a Friend at Midnight" is so similar in format and emphasis that there is little doubt that in it Jesus is making a very similar point about the trustworthiness of God.

(b) Getting acquainted with the text

Once again we have but one text of this parable. Only Luke has preserved it, and this time without any comment as to its meaning. However, by placing it between the Lord's Prayer (Luke 11:1–4) and a series of admonitions to "ask," "seek," and "knock" (Luke 11:9f.) he suggests that this story (like the parable of the Wicked Judge) refers to prayer. It teaches us that we should pray boldly and "not lose heart."

But if again we read the parable, detached from its present literary setting, another emphasis emerges.

> Which of you who has a friend will go to him at midnight and say to him, "Friend, lend me three loaves; for a friend of mine has arrived on a journey, and I have nothing to set before him"; and he will answer from within, "Do not bother me; the door is now shut, and my children are with me in bed; I cannot get up and give you anything"?
>
> I tell you, though he will not get up and give him anything because he is his friend, yet because of his importunity he will rise and give him whatever he needs.

If prayer were the main point of this parable, the focus would be on the man *in need* of bread. But this is not the case. Stress falls on the "friend." "Which of you who has a *friend* . . ." the parable begins. And it concludes with an astute observation about this "friend." As in the case of the parable of the Wicked Judge, the main character is the one petitioned, not the petitioner.

A somewhat technical observation is worth noting at this point. The parable opens with a question ("Which of you . . ."). The form of this question (in Greek) is used only when a strong positive or negative answer is expected. Joachim Jeremias recommends that we translate this idiom as follows: *"Can you imagine . . ."* "Can you imagine anyone having a friend, and going to him at midnight . . ."

This observation heightens our awareness that the focus here is on the "friend," and what might happen should a need arise requiring that this friend be awakened at midnight for help (three loaves of bread). *Can you imagine* that a *friend,* under these circumstances, would respond by shouting from his bed, "Do not bother me . . ."?

Certainly not! No true friend would act in this manner. Why, "I tell you," even were this friend not wanting to get up and open his door and give the bread requested (Jesus adds), he'll do it anyway, just because the petitioner had the nerve to come and make the request ("because of his importunity").

The parable paints a true life situation. It is certainly the way a friend would react, even a not-too-good friend.

(c) Deciding which text to study

There is no decision in this instance, for we have but one text and it raises no problems. We must be careful only to study the parable apart from the verses that precede and follow it. This arrangement of verses is from the hand of Luke and does not necessarily reflect the setting in which Jesus *first* told it (see our earlier discussion on how the Gospels were composed, pp. 10-14).

(d) Meaning in the setting of Jesus' life

No doubt the original reason Jesus told this story was again to awaken confidence toward God. This parable is another one of Jesus' "how much more" teachings. "If you then, who are evil, know how to give good gifts to your children, *how much more* will your Father who is in heaven give good things to those who ask him" (Matt.

11:13). Jesus loved to point from the flickering goodness in man to the greater goodness of God. If we can trust earthly fathers and friends, frail and imperfect as they are, why do we not find it easier to trust God?

(e) Listening to the parables today

Do not forget to memorize the parables just studied. Only when you can retell them will you really begin to grasp their dynamic as stories. (See the suggestions for group study in the Appendix.) What thoughts do they awaken about life today? A few of my musings are the following: Modern men and women, Christian and non-Christian alike, also lack confidence in God. This in fact may be the root crisis of our time, for where a society loses its hold on the reality of a transcendent providence that is good, it loses its hold on life.

A factor in modern skepticism (some would say the chief factor) is the picture of the universe opened up to us by modern science. We are increasingly aware of ourselves as tiny creatures in a cosmic space so vast that we can scarcely measure it. We know now that our history on this fragile planet stretches back millions of years into frightening obscurity. What is the meaning of the short life each of us lives in this mysterious universe?

Observations such as these have led some modern thinkers to the brink of despair. They cannot discover a rational response and conclude that there is none. The highest wisdom, they tell us, is to face openly, honestly and courageously the absurdity of life.

Others with equal candor confront these same awesome facts and questions, but find their thoughts moving in another direction. The well-known sociologist Peter Berger is one of these. In his book *A Rumor of Angels,* he speaks of a child waking in the night surrounded by darkness, alone, and beset by nameless threats. But then the mother takes the child in her arms, cradles it and says in effect: "Don't be afraid. Everything's going to be all right. The world is trustworthy." In this act, says Berger, darkness and fear are banished and "the benign shape of the world" is restored.

Peter Berger asks: Is this universal gesture of motherhood true? Does the mother communicate to her child, in this act of comfort, valid information about life? Or is this simply a lie, perpetrated on the children of the race generation after generation?

Our confidence in God may come to us from many sources. As a Jew Jesus shared that unique revelation of God to Israel of which we can still read in the pages of the Hebrew Bible. As a child he learned, as we do, of the God of Abraham, Moses and the prophets—of that creative intelligence whose face no man has seen, who fashioned the world, but is not of it, and whose dynamic will and love hover over the whole of history. Furthermore, as an adult Jesus' faith was no doubt nourished by uniquely personal experiences, such as the one the Gospels tell us he had at the Jordan in the aftermath of his baptism (Mark 1:10f.).

But it is characteristic of Jesus that he could see signs and hints of the goodness of God not only in the scriptures of his people, not only in personal religious experiences, but in the experiences of daily life. A wicked judge giving in to the pleadings of a poor widow was as much evidence to him of the goodness of God as the story of God's actions on behalf of Israel at the Reed Sea. A friend sacrificing his night's rest to meet the emergency needs of a neighbor pointed to the presence of a higher goodness as surely as a dramatic miracle.

When it comes to faith in God, we are apparently set before inescapable choices. Obviously God does not impose himself upon us in such a way that we are compelled to trust or not trust. *God's presence in history is a hidden presence.* If we end up believing in God and in the meaning of life, it is in part because we have chosen to do so. If we end up disbelieving, this too, in part, is on the basis of our choice. For those who choose to believe in God, there are hints everywhere of his reality and goodness. For those who choose against God, there is no compelling evidence to the contrary. This is what faith is all about.

The parables of Jesus are radiant with the depth of *his* choice and experience. He trusted God and saw his faith confirmed in the everyday world that surrounded him.

Through his parables he invites us to share his decision. They can do no more than that, for trusting God will always require our own personal act of faith. Once made, however, the universe will begin to reveal its hidden message. We will begin to see, as Jesus did, "metaphors" of God's love in unexpected places.

QUESTIONS FOR DISCUSSION
AND FURTHER STUDY:

1. How do I handle my doubts? Discuss both the creative and destructive possibilities of doubting.
2. Why do I believe that God is trustworthy? Why do I question it?
3. What decision have I made about God? How does this decision influence the way I "see" or perceive the world around me?

II. THE COMING OF GOD'S KINGDOM

3. THE BUDDING FIG TREE
(Mark 13:28f./Matt. 24:32f./Luke 21:29–31)

(a) Getting oriented

Luke's version of the Budding Fig Tree speaks of God's Kingdom (Luke 21:31). So also do most of the parables we will be looking at in this section of our study. The Gospels tell us that the proclamation of the nearness of "God's Kingdom" was at the heart of Jesus' message (Mark 1:15). In getting oriented to this group of parables we should consider briefly what he might have meant by these words.

In the time of Jesus the Jewish people were praying the following prayer at the conclusion of their synagogue services:

Exalted and hallowed be his great name in the world which he created according to his will.
May he [God] rule his kingdom in your lifetime and in your days and in the lifetime of the whole house of Israel, speedily and soon.
And to this, say: Amen.

This prayer implies that Jesus' contemporaries thought of God's rule, God's kingdom, as a *future*-coming event. It also indicates with what fervor they were longing for the coming of that kingdom. They wanted it to come "speedily and soon." *What they were hoping for was a dramatic act of divine power that would transform the entire universe at a certain moment in time and make all wrongs right.* This expectation of a world-transforming event ushering in a totally "new age" is sometimes referred to by scholars as "apocalypticism" (meaning "revelationism"). In Jesus' day there were many who thought that the time was near when this would happen, and who were speculating when and how it would all take place (see C. K. Barrett, *N. T. Background*).

Is this what Jesus meant when he spoke of God's kingdom? Was he too an apocalyptic visionary?

In Luke 17:20–21 we read:

Being asked by the Pharisees when the kingdom of God was coming, he answered them, "The kingdom of God is not coming with signs to be observed; nor will they say, 'Lo, here it is!' or 'There!' for behold, the kingdom of God is in the midst of you."

In this scene Jesus is questioned by a group of apocalyptic-minded Pharisees who believed in the future coming of "the kingdom of God." They assumed that Jesus did too. So their only question of him was what his thoughts were as to *when* this mighty event would take place. What cosmic "signs" did he think might warn of its nearness? What unusual events would give evidence of its imminence?

Jesus' answer was surprising. The kingdom of God is not coming "with signs to be observed," he replied. It is "in your midst" (among you). On another occasion he is reported to have said: "If it is by the finger of God that I cast out demons, *then the kingdom of God has come upon you*" (Luke 11:20/Matt. 12:28). *From this it is evident that Jesus believed God's kingdom was not simply a future-coming event, but was already manifesting itself.* It is even now coming "upon you." The healing of a sick man by the "finger" (gentle power) of God is already evidence of it.

Jesus no doubt shared the expectation of his contemporaries that God would one day transform the earth in some unimaginable way (Luke 17:24). But it was not this expectation that preoccupied him. What filled his consciousness was the realization that *already* God's power is at work, transforming the world, *in advance* of that final revelation of God's kingdom upon which the hearts of so many of his contemporaries were set (see George E. Ladd, *The Presence of the Future*).

It is this faith in the presence of God's kingdom that seems to radiate from the parables we are now going to study, and in an especially vivid way in the Budding Fig Tree, the Leaven, and the Mustard Seed.

(b) Getting acquainted with the texts

For the first time in this study we are confronted by more than one text. The differences between them are not great, but worth noting nevertheless.

Matt. 24:32–33	Mark 13:28–29	Luke 21:29–31
From the fig tree learn its lesson: as soon as its branch becomes tender and puts forth its leaves, you know that summer is near. So also when you see all these things you know that he is near, at the very gates.	From the fig tree learn its lesson: as soon as its branch becomes tender and puts forth its leaves, you know that summer is near. So also when you see these things taking place, you know that he is near, at the very gates.	And he told them a parable: Look at the fig tree, and all the trees; as soon as they come out in leaf, you see for yourselves and know that the summer is already near. So also when you see these things taking place, you know that the kingdom of God is near.

If Matthew copied his version of this parable from Mark, as most scholars think (see above, "Why differing versions of the same parable?"), it is apparent that he did so almost word for word. Only his final sentence varies slightly.

Luke's version, on the other hand, departs so markedly from both Matthew and Mark that we must speculate that he drew it from another source. His text asks us to look not only at "the fig tree" but "all the trees." It emphasizes the point that when they put forth their leaves "you see for yourselves" that summer is "already" near. And most striking of all, his version specifies that the comparison here is to "the kingdom of God." "So also when you see these things taking place, you know that the *kingdom of God* is near."

In all three versions the stress falls on a comparison between trees blossoming and "these things." As the one is a sign of summer coming, the other gives notice that "he is near . . ." (Matthew, Luke), "the kingdom of God is near" (Luke). But what is meant by "these things"? And of what are "these things" a portent?

If we were to study this parable in its present *literary* context, the answers to these questions would be apparent. "These things" that are to be "seen" would be the "signs" in sun, moon and stars (Luke 21:25) of the advent of the "Son of man" at the close of the age (Mark 13:26). However, in Luke 17:21 (as noted above) Jesus taught that the end of the age is not coming with "signs to be observed." *If this is truly a parable of Jesus, it is not likely that he told it to encourage cosmic "sign"-watching. Furthermore, a gently budding fig tree is not a very apt symbol for the frightening planetary and terrestrial upheavals referred to in the preceding verses.*

But there is another possibility in interpreting this parable. If we ignore its literary context, which stems from the early church, and imagine this parable to be one that Jesus told *originally* in the context of his Galilean ministry, then (following Luke's version) this could be understood as a parable of the "nearness" of God's kingdom *as a present reality.* "These things" that the disciples are to "see" would be then not cosmic "signs," but the gentle exorcisms, healings, and conversions taking place in and around the ministry of Jesus.

It is possible, then, that the parable of the Budding Fig Tree was initially told (roughly as in Luke) with reference to the kingdom of God being "near" right now; it was retold by the early Christians with reference to Jesus' second coming (". . . he is near, at the very gates").

(c) Deciding which text to study

Luke's version of this parable, with its final reference to the kingdom of God being near, would appear to be the earlier version of this parable, for this is typically the language and message of Jesus. But his ". . . and all the trees" (in addition to the fig tree) looks like a secondary expansion. The fig tree is commonplace in Palestine and especially striking in the spring when its budding green leaves sprout on its bare, dark branches. It is apparent why Jesus would have singled out this tree especially (and not all the trees) as a parable of the nearness of God's gently "budding" kingdom.

(d) Meaning in the setting of Jesus' life

Jesus experienced God as active in the universe that he had made. While others debated "when" the kingdom of God would come, he proclaimed that it was already "in your midst." "*Today* this scripture has been fulfilled in your hearing" (Luke 4:21).

Jesus wanted to share this way of experiencing life with his disciples. Look at the fig tree, he said. See how it shoots forth its buds and leaves in spring. That tells you that summer is near. In just the same way, when you see "these things" (healing, repentance) taking place you should know and believe that God's kingdom is near, yes, in your very midst. ". . . In the new spiritual life burgeoning through the ministry of Jesus a sign [is given] of the day of salvation" (Beare).

We will postpone our discussion of the relevance of this parable for today until after we have looked at the next two closely related parables about Leaven and Mustard Seed.

4. THE LEAVEN
(Matt. 13:33/Luke 13:20f./Thomas 96)

(a) Getting oriented

All that was said by way of introducing the parable of the Budding Fig Tree must be kept in mind as we study the parables of Leaven and Mustard Seed. They too are parables of the "kingdom of God." Their intent is to evoke awareness of what Jesus meant by these joyful words.

(b) Getting acquainted with the texts

In addition to the versions of this parable in Matthew and Luke, we should also acquaint ourselves with its text in the Gospel of

Thomas. About half of the 114 sayings of Jesus recorded in this recently discovered Gnostic manuscript are similar to sayings in the Gospels. Among them are twelve parables; and the parable of the Leaven is one of them.

Matt. 13:33	Luke 13:20–21	Thomas 96
The kingdom of heaven is like leaven which a woman took and hid in three measures of meal, till it was all leavened.	To what shall I compare the kingdom of God: It is like leaven which a woman took and hid in three measures of meal, till it was all leavened.	Jesus [said]: The Kingdom of the Father is like a woman who took a little leaven and [hid] it in meal; she made large loaves of it. He that hath ears, let him hear.

The focus of all three texts is on the everyday marvel of a woman at work baking bread. In doing so she handles a large batch of dough. Matthew and Luke tell us that it was "three measures," or about fifty pounds, enough to feed 100 people (Jeremias). Thomas says that the loaves were "large." And so the accent falls on the "little leaven" (Thomas) that this woman placed in a *large* mass of dough and how, in the course of time, it leavened the entire substance (Matthew, Luke).

An important point in the translation of this parable should be noted here. The phrase "is like" is not meant to suggest a direct correspondence between "kingdom of God" and "leaven" (Matthew, Luke), nor between the kingdom of the Father and the "woman" (Thomas). Rather, it refers to the entire action described. On the basis of the Aramaic construction lying behind this phrase, Joachim Jeremias suggests that wherever this word usage is found we should translate: "It is the case with the kingdom of God as with . . ."

(c) Deciding which text to study

The minor variations between the three texts are not too significant. The synoptic versions, however, center our attention on the great mass of dough, slowly rising because of a tiny bit of leaven hidden away in it. Thomas distracts from this picture by shifting, at the end, away from the leaven and dough to the large loaves. The synoptic versions are preferable.

(d) Meaning in the setting of Jesus' life

One must again recall the feverish speculations among many of Jesus' contemporaries regarding the mighty, world-transforming *future*-coming kingdom of God. By way of contrast Jesus points to the miracle of leaven in dough. Although not always visible or tangible, he seems to be saying, God's power already penetrates deep into the realities of everyday life.

5. THE MUSTARD SEED
(Mark 4:30–32/Matt. 13:31f./Luke 13:18f./Thomas 20)

(a) Getting oriented

In Matthew and Luke the parables of Leaven and Mustard Seed are grouped together. The reason is apparent. Both parables speak of something very small working silently to produce something strikingly large. Both are parables of the kingdom of God.

(b) Getting acquainted with the texts

No less than four versions of the parable of the Mustard Seed are available for study. The differences between them are numerous for so short a text.

Mark's version of this parable is slightly longer than the others, mostly because of phrases (not appearing in the other versions) that exaggerate the contrast between the tiny seed and the large shrub ("the smallest of all the seeds on earth ... the greatest of all shrubs"). In Luke the seed was "sowed in his garden" (something strictly forbidden in Palestine); in Matthew it is sown in a "field"; in Mark "upon the ground"; in Thomas it fell (grew wild?) "on the tilled earth." The "shrub" (Mark, Matt.) is called "a tree" in Luke, "a large branch" in Thomas. The birds make "nests in its branches"

Matt. 13:31–32

Another parable he put before them, saying, "The kingdom of heaven is like a grain of mustard seed which a man took and sowed in his field; it is the smallest of all seeds, but when it has grown it is the greatest of shrubs and becomes a tree, so that the birds of the air come and make nests in its branches."

Mark 4:30–32

And he said, "With what can we compare the kingdom of God, or what parable shall we use for it? It is like a grain of mustard seed, which when sown upon the ground, is the smallest seed of all the seeds on earth; yet when it is sown it grows up and becomes the greatest of all shrubs, and puts forth large branches, so that the birds of the air can make nests in its shade."

Luke 13:18–19

He said therefore, "What is the kingdom of God like? And to what shall I compare it? It is like a grain of mustard seed which a man took and sowed in his garden; and it grew and became a tree, and the birds of the air made nests in its branches."

Thomas 20

The disciples said to Jesus: Tell us what the kingdom of heaven is like. He said to them: It is like a grain of mustard seed, smaller than all seeds; but when it falls on the earth which is tilled, it puts forth a great branch, and becomes shelter for the birds of heaven.

(according to Matthew and Luke), "in its shade" (according to Mark). In Thomas they find "shelter."

Actually the mustard seed does not grow into a "tree." It is an annual shrub, growing as high as eight feet. If birds flock to it, it is not to build nests, but to find shelter in its shade (Mark, Thomas).

Why then do some of the versions speak of a "tree" and "nests"? In Ezekiel 17:23 "tree" is used as an image of the future coming of God's kingdom. Birds flock to it and build nests in its branches (see also Daniel 4:10ff.). Among certain Jewish apocalyptic circles this was understood to be a symbol of the Gentiles "flocking" to the kingdom of God at the close of the age. The early Christians (who were deeply influenced by Jewish thinking about the future) told and retold the Mustard Seed parable in this light. As they did so the shrub became the tree-symbol of Ezekiel 17:23 and Daniel 4:10.

(c) Deciding which text to study

Thomas seems to have the simplest version of this parable. Originally the parable may have been about a wild mustard seed that fell on the earth and grew into a shrub large enough for birds to find shelter. Statements in several versions that emphasize either the smallness of the seed or the "tree"-like size of the shrub are probably due to tendencies among the early Christians to interpret this parable in the light of familiar apocalyptic imagery.

(d) Meaning in the setting of Jesus' life

Jesus' contemporaries were expecting the kingdom of God as a future upheaval that would end the present age. But again Jesus portrays the kingdom otherwise. Something powerful is *already* at work in our world. Look at what happens when a tiny mustard seed falls to the ground. In one season it grows into a bush so large that birds can find shelter in its shade. This astonishing plant with its rapid growth is, for Jesus, a metaphorical event, pointing to the power of God already at work "in your midst." God's "reign has invaded human history in advance of the eschatological consummation" (Ladd).

(e) Listening to the parables today

Don't forget to memorize and retell the parables and discuss the thoughts they awaken in you. The importance of this step cannot be emphasized too much (see suggestions for group study in the Appendix). Here are a few things that I "hear" as I try to listen to the three parables we have just studied:

Jesus was deeply conscious of "God" at work in human affairs. That comes through powerfully in every parable we have looked at so far. And yet the events to which he pointed as evidence of this were not such as to compel conversion to his point of view.

Whether God is trustworthy (as noted in the previous section of our study) is by no means self-evident. No less is it self-evident that God's kingdom is present "in our midst." It requires a choice. "Faith," writes a contemporary theologian, "is ... the adoption of a fundamental stance in life ... the choice of a basic attitude to reality" (Charles Davis, *Temptations of Religion*). This choice, he continues, is not attained nor retained "through conceptual analysis," but "through a personal, self-involving response."

Modern science has extended the range of our vision outward, backward and inward. We have today at our disposal a far greater range of facts about the origins and development of life, the course of human history, the nature of the universe, and of the human psyche than any other generation. But the accumulation of facts has not diminished the ambivalent character of human existence. One man looks at these facts and sees a frightening array of chance configurations, signifying nothing. Another looks at them and sees them aglow with divine purpose.

A modern example of this latter is the priest-paleontologist, Teilhard de Chardin. For many decades Christians resisted the frightening picture of the universe that was gradually coming into sight through modern science. That the earth swings in a dark and foreboding space around the sun, that billions of years preceded the appearance of man on this planet—where in such a universe are we to see the handiwork of God so fervently proclaimed in our scriptures?

Teilhard writes as one who has found the answer. He speaks of a world in constant process of being changed and transformed by the grace of God. "We are sometimes inclined to think" he says at the conclusion of his devotional masterpiece, *The Divine Milieu,* "that the same things are monotonously repeated over and over again in the history of creation. That is because the season is too long by comparison with the brevity of our individual lives, and the transformation too vast and too inward by comparison with our superficial and restricted outlook, for us to see the progress of what is tirelessly taking place in and through all matter and all spirit."

These sentences catch the mood of Jesus who saw in the actions of the worst of men parables of the love of God, and in the ordinary events of nature parables of the purposeful activity of God. A small seed that sprouts into a great bush, a bit of leaven in the midst of a mass of dough, tender green leaves suddenly blossoming on the gnarled skin of a fig tree were symbolic to him of a beneficent power active in the universe in many other ways.

Whether we choose to share his vision of God's kingdom is up to us. Evidence to the contrary there no doubt is. But for those who choose to open themselves to this vision, there are also validating experiences. A man healed of psychic disturbance, a small child in its untrammeled humility, a crusty tax collector at last ready to face up to his cruel avarice—in these and other events of this kind Jesus felt the powers of the coming age of salvation (Luke 19:9). Similar things continue to happen in our time, pointing the way to the possible meaning of the human experiment and its ultimate destiny.

QUESTIONS FOR DISCUSSION
AND FURTHER STUDY:

1. Do you see the activity of God in the affairs of our time? Where?
2. Are you an optimist or a pessimist? Why?

III. IN THE FACE OF DIFFICULTIES

6. THE PATIENT FARMER (Mark 4:26–29)

(a) Getting oriented

If Jesus proclaimed the goodness of God and saw about him evidence of God at work, it was not because he was oblivious to the dark side of life. Such an "escapist" attitude would in any case have been difficult, for he lived not in good times but in extremely bad times. His people suffered under the boot of military occupation by Rome.

Many of his contemporaries grew impatient with this oppressive and humiliating situation and drifted toward strategies of violence. If God was silent and withdrawn, if he did nothing for the deliverance of his people, they thought, perhaps it was because he waited for something on their part. Perhaps what was missing was action like that of the Israelite leaders of old, who dared to summon the armies of God's people into battle against the foe in the face of overwhelming odds, because they knew (at the critical moment) God would help them (see David M. Rhoads, *Israel in Revolution, 6–74 C.E.*).

Despair and smoldering militancy lie in the background of the next parables we will study.

(b) Getting acquainted with the text

Only Mark has the text of this parable. Why Matthew and Luke when compiling their Gospels rejected it is a mystery.

Mark 4:26–29

The kingdom of God is as if a man should scatter seed upon the ground, and should sleep and rise night and day,

and the seed should sprout and grow, he knows not how.

The earth produces of itself, first the blade, then the ear, then the full grain in the ear.

But when the grain is ripe, at once he puts in the sickle, because the harvest has come.

The final sentence echoes the command in Joel 3:13: "Put in the sickle for the harvest is ripe." In Joel these words refer to the judgment of nations in the "Valley of Jehoshaphat." But that is clearly not their meaning here. Nor does the parable even focus on the harvest so much as on events taking place *before* harvest: sowing, confident waiting, spontaneous (mysterious) growth, and eventually "the full grain in the ear."

(c) Deciding which text to study

There is no choice in this instance but to study the parable as it appears in Mark.

(d) Meaning in the setting of Jesus' life

Like the parables of Leaven and Mustard Seed, this one speaks of something small quietly producing significant results. The kingdom of God is already active "in your midst!"

But there is a new element here. *The focus of this parable is not*

so much on the seed as on the sower. With economy of words we are
told of a farmer who scatters seed and then waits, through many
days (sleeping and rising, night and day) while the seed slowly
sprouts and grows, "he knows not how." "Of itself" *(aùtomátē)* the
earth produces the plant, blade, ear, and finally the grain.

Jesus may have spoken this parable with special reference to the
Zealots, a militant revolutionary group in Judaism. The Zealots were
impatient. They were tired of the misery into which the Jews had
fallen as a result of the Roman occupation. They were tired of waiting year in and year out for God to act on Israel's behalf. They wanted to hasten the coming of God's kingdom by a militant uprising.
Gamaliel speaks of these Zealots in his speech to the Jewish Sanhe-
drin in Acts 5:35ff. and mentions two of their fallen leaders by name
(again see David M. Rhoads, *Israel in Revolution 6–74 C. E.*).

At least one of Jesus' disciples was a Zealot sympathizer (Luke
6:15). There may have been others. Even Simon Peter may have initially thought of Jesus as a Zealot-type leader (Mark 8:32).

In the parable of the Patient Farmer Jesus presents an alterna-
tive to Zealotism. He does not deny the need for something new. In
the face of misery and suffering, revolutionary changes are indeed
called for. *But those who would hasten the coming of God's kingdom
by military measures have no respect for the "mysteries of growth."*
The farmer, not the soldier, is the authentic metaphorical model of
the man who fosters the kingdom.

Before discussing the significance of this parable for today, let's
look at the closely related parable of the Weeds Among the Wheat.

7. WEEDS AMONG THE WHEAT
(Matt. 13:24–30/Thomas 57)

(a) Getting oriented

Like the parable of the patient farmer this one also tells of a
man sowing seed in supreme confidence that it will grow and produce grain.

(b) Getting acquainted with the texts

The texts of the parable of the Weeds Among the Wheat pose a double problem. As previously, we must get acquainted with the texts of the parable itself. In addition, in this instance we must come to terms with an allegorical explanation of the parable recorded in Matthew 13:36–43.

In order to assess the value of the allegory as an interpretation, the parable itself must be studied first of all in its own right.

Only Matthew among the synoptics records this parable, but a somewhat shortened version appears in the Gospel according to Thomas. A comparison of the two is instructive.

Matt. 13:24–30	Thomas 57
The kingdom of heaven may be compared to a man who sowed good seed in his field; but while men were sleeping, his enemy came and sowed weeds among the wheat, and went away.	The kingdom of the Father is like a man who had [good] seed. His enemy came by night, he sowed a weed among the good seed.
So when the plants came up and bore grain, then the weeds appeared also.	
And the servants of the householder came and said to him, "Sir, did you not sow good seed in your field? How then has it weeds?"	
He said to them, "An enemy has done this."	
The servants said to him, "Then do you want us to go and gather them?"	
But he said, "No; lest in gathering the weeds you root up the wheat along with them.	The man did not allow them to pull up the weed. He said to them: Lest perhaps you go to pull up the weed, and pull up the wheat with it. For on the day of harvest the weeds will be manifest; they will be pulled up and burned.
Let both grow together until the harvest; and at harvest time I will tell the reapers, 'Gather the weeds first and bind them in bundles to be burned, but gather the wheat into my barn.' "	

Matthew's version centers on the "man who sowed good seed in his field" and the manner in which he resolved a very critical problem: the presence of an unusual crop of weeds among the wheat. "How did such a thing happen?" the servants want to know. The farmer has a hunch that "an enemy has done this." But what then should be done? The servants want to destroy the weeds immediately by pulling them out, but the householder says: "No, lest in gathering the weeds you root up the wheat along with them. *Let both grow together until harvest.*" That seems to be the climactic word. At harvest time the weeds can be safely gathered into bundles (for fuel?) and the wheat gathered into the barn.

The Thomas version of this parable looks like a summary of the Matthew text. As summaries go it is not a very good one. It displays a definite bias. It drops completely the dialogue between master and servants. It also omits the crucial advice: "Let both grow together until harvest," and ends the parable short of the phrase that speaks of gathering the wheat "into the barn." In this way the focus of the parable is shifted away from the advice of the farmer to the fate of the weeds.

Matthew's version, then, is by far the preferable one and paints a rather vivid picture of a farmer facing a crisis in a very wise and confident way. He will not allow his enemy to frighten him into precipitous, foolish action. Weeds and wheat are allowed to mature together. Separating them can best be done at harvest time. The slaves who want to tear out the weeds at once are told to be patient out of regard for the wheat.

We are in a position now to look at the allegorical interpretation of this parable in Matthew 13:36–43 and to evaluate it. The setting is a "house" away from the "crowds" where Jesus is together with his "disciples" (v. 36). These disciples ask for an explanation of "the parable of the weeds in the field." That they call it the parable of the "weeds" already betrays a shift of focus (similar to that in Thomas).

The allegory follows (vv. 37ff.) beginning with an allegorical code:

He who sows the good seed is the Son of man;
The field is the world,
    and the good seed means the sons of the kingdom;

the weeds are the sons of the evil one,
and the enemy who sowed them is the devil;
the harvest is the close of the age,
and the reapers are angels.

The allegory proper begins then at verse 40:

Just as the weeds are gathered and burned with fire, so will it be at the close of the age. The Son of Man will send his angels and they will gather out of his kingdom all causes of sin and all evil-doers, and throw them into the furnace of fire; there men will weep and gnash their teeth. Then the righteous will shine like the sun in the kingdom of their Father. He who has ears, let him hear.

Before commenting on this particular allegory, it might be useful to say a few words about allegories in general (see above "How do parables work?"). What is an allegory? One way of answering this question is to note the way an allegory differs from a parable. The differences are apparent at two points especially. First of all, a parable generally has a single major symbolic thrust or meaning. An allegory on the other hand attaches symbolic meaning to virtually every major item of the story being told. Secondly, the meaning of a parable although subtle is there to be grasped by anyone who listens to it attentively. The meaning of an allegory, however, is often "hidden" and has to be explained by the one who composed it. These distinctions are not hard and fast but point rather to contrasting accents in the two modes of comparing.

The allegorical interpretation under discussion graphically illustrates these two points. No less than seven items in the story of the Weeds Among the Wheat are singled out as having symbolic significance: the sower, the field, the good seed, the weeds, the enemy, the harvest, and the reapers. But exactly what their significance might be is not apparent. Therefore, we are told, Jesus had to explain to his disciples that these refer to the Son of man, the world, the sons of the kingdom, the sons of the evil one, the devil, the close of the age, and the angels. The disciples must also be informed that the purpose of the parable is to present a veiled but detailed description of events that will take place "at the close of the age."

But is this really what the parable was originally all about? A question arises when we note that the parable itself devotes far more attention to the dialogue between farmer and servants over what to do about the weeds than it does to the harvest scene (on which the allegory concentrates its attention). The crisis that arose when the weeds were first discovered, the conversation between master and servants over what to do, the farmer's decisive counsel to be patient and let both weeds and wheat grow together until harvest—*all this is completely by-passed by the allegorical interpretation.* "Just as the weeds are gathered and burned with fire, so will it be at the close of the age." These are the words with which the allegorical interpretation begins.

This lack of correspondence between the thrust of the parable and the focus of the allegory is one reason why questions have been raised by Biblical scholars as to whether this allegory does in fact come from Jesus. Would Jesus have interpreted his own parable in this manner? The question becomes even more acute when we note more precisely the terms used in the allegory. Joachim Jeremias (who has studied this matter in detail) has drawn up a list of no less than thirty-seven words and phrases in this short passage that are characteristic of "Matthew" but not of Jesus. Jesus, for example, does not elsewhere call his followers "sons of the kingdom," never refers to "angels" of the Son of Man, and never speaks of the "kingdom" of the Son of Man, as the allegory does. On the other hand, these can be shown to be Matthean ideas and emphases.

Observations of this kind have compelled virtually every contemporary student of the parables to conclude that the allegorical interpretation of the parable of the Weeds Among the Wheat does not come from Jesus. Joachim Jeremias thinks it might have been composed by "Matthew" himself, using the allegorical interpretation of the Sower as a pattern. If so, it is an instructive example of early Christian teaching. It is not however a teaching of Jesus, nor an accurate guide to what he may have originally meant to say in telling the parable of the Weeds Among the Wheat. Allegory in general is not the right approach to the interpretation of the original meaning of Jesus' parables.

This conclusion (which has been remarkably confirmed by the Gospel of Thomas, where the allegories are all missing) is the foundation of modern parable study, but it is one that may startle those who are becoming acquainted with the Gospels for the first time. Many Christians assume that whatever is found in the Gospels must be taken at face value. Where a teaching is stated as being a teaching of Jesus, that is what it is.

Detailed study, however, over many decades has proven otherwise. We must bear in mind that in assembling the Gospels, the Gospel editors were not guided by the rules of history-writing that control the work of modern historians. Distinctions between original sources and later interpretations were not nearly so rigidly maintained. It was quite customary, for example, for Greek historians of that period to put into the mouths of the persons they were writing about speeches composed by the historians themselves. For an editor of Jesus' teachings to put into his mouth a parabolic interpretation that had arisen in the Christian church, or one that he himself might have composed, was a procedure that would have been quite acceptable and understood far differently in that day than today.

(c) Deciding which text to study

Both Thomas and the Matthean allegory misconstrue somewhat the original parable. Matthew 13:24–30, without reference to the allegory in 13:37ff., is the text to be studied if we want to know what *Jesus* intended to communicate through this story.

(d) Meaning in the setting of Jesus' life

Should the weeds be pulled out before harvest time? That is the crucial question posed by this parable. The answer of the farmer is straightforward: "No, lest in gathering the weeds you root up the wheat as well. Let both grow together until the harvest." He is supremely confident in the power of the wheat to survive, even when threatened by an extraordinary growth of weeds.

Even more explicit than in the previous parable is the reference here to the impatience that characterized the Jewish revolutionaries of Jesus' day. The servants in the story want to "go and gather" the weeds at once and be rid of them.

If on the one hand Jesus had to protect his vision of God's kingdom from distortion by those who would hear it in futuristic, apocalyptic terms, he had to protect it, on the other, from those who would see it as a program of precipitous military action. *His experience of God's kingdom was neither apocalyptic nor militant.* Neither a smashing of history by God nor a forceful assault on history by man is his vision of the road ahead for his people.

No, there is another way. Jesus recognizes the difficulties. He too sees the spreading evil that everywhere seems to threaten the good. But his confidence remains unshaken in the power of God to produce something on earth. An impatient, clumsy attack on evil will hurt the good as much as the evil. The right way is the way of the wise farmer who trusts his crop to survive until harvest.

Again we will wait until we have dealt with the next parable before discussing the significance of this group of stories for today.

8. THE SOWER
(Mark 4:3–8/Matt. 13:3–8/Luke 8:5–8/Thomas 9)

(a) Getting oriented

Still a third parable (the Sower) centers on the farmer sowing seed. In the parable of the Patient Farmer, the focus as we have seen was on the farmer's relaxed confidence in the mystery of growth. "Weeds Among Wheat" described a special problem that emerged for a particular farmer during the time of growth (too many weeds). In the parable of the Sower, it is the sowing process itself and its consequences that capture our attention.

(b) Getting acquainted with the texts

A thorough comparison of the four available texts of this parable is beyond the scope of our present study. It will simplify matters if we begin where several recent investigators end, with the conclusion that Mark 4:1-9 is the earliest version of this parable, and that this text was in turn one of the versions used by Matthew and the only text known to Luke.

We also have an allegorical interpretation of this parable to evaluate (Mark 4:13-20/Matt. 13:18-23/Luke 8:11-15).

Our procedure will be the same as the one followed in the preceding parable: first look at the parable without any reference to the allegorical interpretation, and then examine the allegory to see whether it actually does capture the thrust of the original story.

We shall begin then by looking at the parable itself.

Assuming that Mark (as suggested above) has, by and large, preserved the earliest version of this parable, it is noteworthy that two features of Mark's text are unique.

First of all, only Mark's telling of the parable maintains a sharp distinction between the seed (singular) that was sown on the path, the rocky ground, and among the thorns, and the "other seeds" (plural) that fell on good soil ("some seed . . . other seed . . . other seed . . . other seeds"). *In Mark the parable has to do not so much with four types of soil as with the fate of two groups of seed.*

Another feature of Mark's version of the story is the phrase (at the end of the description of the fate of the third type of seed): "And it yielded no grain." This statement closes off the first part of the parable. Neither the seed sown along the path, nor that which dropped on rocky ground, nor that which fell among thorns bore any fruit. This then is in sharp contrast to the "seeds" that fell on good soil and yielded bountifully.

Mark's parable of the Sower draws a contrast between seed that produced no grain and seeds that, falling on good soil, produced a rich harvest. (I am indebted to Crossan for this and the following observations.)

One might ask: If Matthew and Luke copied their version of this parable from Mark, why did they omit these two details? Possibly they were already too strongly influenced by the allegorical interpretation of this parable, where the accent is more on the four different types of soil than on the fate of the two groups of seed.

While Mark then preserves the basic structure of this parable more clearly than the others, there is one point where his text is a

Matt. 13:3-9	Mark 4:3-9	Luke 8:5-8	Thomas 9
A sower went out to sow. And as he sowed, some seeds fell along the path, and the birds came and devoured them. Other seeds fell on rocky ground, where they had not much soil, and immediately they sprang up, since they had no depth of soil, but when the sun rose they were scorched; and since they had no root they withered away. Other seeds fell upon thorns, and the thorns grew up and choked them.	Listen! A sower went out to sow. And as he sowed, some seed fell along the path, and the birds came and devoured it. Other seed fell on rocky ground, where it had not much soil, and immediately it sprang up, since it had no depth of soil; and when the sun rose it was scorched, and since it had no root it withered away. Other seed fell among thorns and the thorns grew up and choked it, and it yielded no grain.	A sower went out to sow his seed; and as he sowed, some fell along the path, and was trodden under foot, and the birds of the air devoured it. And some fell on the rock; and as it grew up, it withered away, because it had no moisture. And some fell among the thorns; and the thorns grew with it and choked it.	Behold, the sower went forth, he filled his hand, he cast. Some fell upon the road; the birds came, and gathered them. Others fell on the rock, and sent no root down to the earth, nor did they sprout any ear up to heaven. And others fell on the thorns; they choked the seed, and the worm ate them.
Other seeds fell on good soil and brought forth grain, some a hundredfold, some sixty, some thirty. He who has ears to hear, let him hear.	And other seeds fell into good soil and brought forth grain, growing up and increasing and yielding thirtyfold and sixtyfold and a hundredfold. And he said, "He who has ears to hear, let him hear."	And some fell into good soil and grew and yielded a hundredfold. And as he said this, he called out, "He who has ears to hear, let him hear."	And others fell on the good earth, and brought forth good fruit unto heaven, some sixty-fold and some an hundred and twentyfold.

bit confusing. The description of the seed that fell on rocky ground is much longer than other parts of the story. Three times we are told that this seed "had not much soil . . . it had no depth of soil . . . it had no root . . . " This is certainly repetitious in an otherwise tersely told tale. But most of all it is rather unclear just what happened to the seed in this case. One set of images suggests that the seed fell on bare rock, and then when the next day's sun arose, it was scorched. The other image suggests that it took root in shallow rocky soil, grew quickly, and then withered away.

Luke obviously sensed the problem here and dealt with it by omitting entirely (in his version) the reference to the sun, choosing instead the image of the seed that grew to a certain point in rocky soil, then withered away "because it had no moisture." Again, however, his choice may have been dictated by the allegorical interpretation that sees here a symbol of those who hear the word and "immediately receive it with joy," but only "for a while." As soon as persecution comes they fall away, because "they have no root in themselves" (Mark 4:16f.). Leaving the allegory to one side, the other picture is equally possible: "Other seed fell on rocky ground . . . and when the sun rose it was scorched." It never even began to grow. (This also is the way Thomas represents it.)

What then is there to say about the allegory in Mark 4:13ff. (and parallels)? As allegories go, one must admit first of all that this one is quite apt. It certainly does not bypass the thrust of this parable to the same degree that the allegory of the "Weeds" missed the point of the parable of the weeds among the wheat. But here too the focus has been shifted from the two types of seed to the four types of soil, and from the contrast between no-fruit and much-fruit to the contrasts between four types of "hearers" (Christians). As in most allegories incidental features of the parable are invested with meaning. It is again doubtful that Jesus interpreted his own parable in this way. Careful analysis of the vocabulary of the allegory (as in the case of the allegory of the "Weeds") points to the early church (rather than Jesus) as the source. To mention just one example: Jesus never speaks of "the word." On the other hand, this way of referring to the Gospel message appears frequently in the vocabulary of the early church (Luke 1:2; Acts 4:4, 6:4, 8:4, etc.).

(c) Deciding which text to study

The suggestion that the allegory is not from Jesus but rather illustrates the way the early Christians began applying this parable to their situation does not mean it is without value.

Our interest in this study, however, is on the meaning of the parable in the setting of Jesus' life. For that purpose the Markan text is our best resource (reading the verse describing the fate of the seed that fell on rocky ground as follows: "Other seed fell on rocky ground . . . and when the sun rose it was scorched . . . ").

(d) Meaning in the setting of Jesus' life

Joachim Jeremias and others inform us that the Palestinian farmer in Jesus' day first sowed, then ploughed his land. This of course is just the opposite of agricultural methods today.

Where the field is first sown, then ploughed, a certain portion of the seed is naturally lost. There are footpaths running through the fields, worn hard by use during the time that the field lay barren. There are rocky sections. There are places where clumps of thorn bushes have sprouted.

To the Palestinian farmer it is all the more a miracle that with all these obstacles and losses, year after year there is a harvest. That of course is due to the fact that amidst the rocks and thorns there is "good soil."

It's not clear what is meant in the parable by "thirtyfold, sixtyfold and a hundredfold." If this refers to the total yield of a given piece of land, the figures are very high. An average crop was tenfold (according to Jeremias). But this could also refer to the ratio between the seed sown and the number of seeds on a given stalk. In that case the yields mentioned would be very good, but no greater than one might expect.

The parable thus describes in terse, rhythmic lines a scene familiar to Jesus' contemporaries: the farmer sowing his field in the fall of the year (just before the winter rains). Jesus saw in this ordinary event a metaphor.

Of what?

There is an obvious note of optimism here (as in all the "farming" stories he told)—a mood of confidence in the powerful, fruitful working of that which at first appears fragile and threatened. This is a kingdom parable as surely as the others we have studied.

But certain difficulties are hinted at. Some of the seed sown is lost. Some of the seed does not take root, grow and bear fruit. Yes, some of the seed is wasted, *but the greater part of the seeds fall on good soil* and produces magnificently.

To what does all this refer? In this instance hardly to the Zealots (as in the case of the Patient Farmer or the Weeds Among Wheat). To whom then?

We cannot be sure, but a possibility would be that in the background here is the growing hostility toward Jesus on the part of the Jewish religious elite (about which we will have much to say in the next section of our study). This hostility must have been discouraging to Jesus' first followers, causing some of them to turn away. To those who remained Jesus may have said: "Look at the Sower and what happens to his seed!" Even though some seed is lost, he is not discouraged, because he knows that by far the greater part of his seed will fall on good soil and will eventually produce a bountiful harvest. Let the farmer sowing teach you to have confidence in the "kingdom of God," in spite of opposition.

(e) Listening to the parables today

Again the important thing is for you to "hear" these parables and identify the thoughts that well up within you as you do. A few thoughts of my own are the following:

The three parables just studied continue the theme touched on by all the parables looked at thus far: confidence in God and awareness of his presence among us now in gracious activity.

But they are also unique. They hint at difficulties that threaten this confidence. *We may classify the difficulties alluded to in a two-fold manner: impatience and discouragement.* The Zealots to whom two of these parables might refer were impatient. They wanted to see God's kingdom realized fully at once and were ready to take drastic action to that end. Others were discouraged because of a lack of response to Jesus' message on the part of the Jewish establishment.

Zealot impatience is still with us in the modern world. It shows its face in every "violent" effort, every attempt to take history "by storm," every belligerent attack on life in order to move it forward beyond the pace of man or God.

The two "farmer" parables call us away from this impatience to inner quietness. They invite us to keep our eyes focused on reality, on the universe as it is, and on the way God works within it. Look at the farmer, how patiently he goes about his life, rising and sleeping, night and day, while the seed is growing. Yes, how confident he is, even when faced by an overgrowth of weeds. That is how we should transact the business of life—trusting God in the face of difficulties.

But impatience has a near relative and it too is ever present in the modern age: discouragement. Instead of reacting with militant fervor toward the difficulties that confront us, we may be tempted to give up. This mood can also cloak itself in piety. There are Christians and Christian groups who speak often and much of the evils of our age, of the times getting worse and worse. They may even justify talk like this on the basis of scripture itself, referring constantly to those texts that speak of catastrophic wickedness engulfing the world. Only a smashing intervention of God into history will save it, they insist. Apart from this the world is hopeless.

There is of course evil in the world. Jesus saw that too. And he warned of troubled days ahead for his people, should they persist in their narrow-minded sectarianism. But even in the midst of all this, he was not pessimistic about the presence of God's kingdom or its future. That is why the parables we have just studied are still so relevant. We still need the good news to which they try to awaken us: Do not be impatient. Do not be discouraged. God is at work. In the midst of everything, there is ample evidence of a gracious, divine activity, if we are but open to see it.

QUESTIONS FOR DISCUSSION AND FURTHER STUDY:

1. Can you recite from memory the parables already studied?
2. Are you more prone to impatience or to discouragement? Or both? Why?
3. How do you react to difficult problems? What part does your faith (or lack of it) play in your response?

PART TWO

PARABLES EVOKING AWARENESS OF A MORE GENUINE GOODNESS

You shall love your neighbor as yourself (Mark 12:31/Matt. 22:39/Luke 10:27).

IV. COMPASSION

9. THE LOST SHEEP
(Matt. 18:12–14/Luke 15:4–7/Thomas 107)

(a) Getting oriented

The parables in the previous section all had to do with our relation to God. We turn now to eleven parables whose theme is interpersonal attitudes. Several of these are among the best known and best loved of Jesus' stories. All of them testify to the way Jesus experienced God as a summons to a new way of thinking and relating to others.

"The time is fulfilled, and the kingdom of God is at hand; repent, and believe in the gospel" (Mark 1:15). This, Mark says, is the substance of what Jesus came preaching in Galilee.

But what, more precisely, does it mean to "repent"? Where we are truly in touch with "God," how will we think and live? The answer can be stated quite simply: "You shall love your neighbor as yourself" (Mark 12:31). But the outworking of this answer in concrete situations often escapes us.

So it was with Jesus' contemporaries. Strongly committed as many of them were to God and the doing of God's will (Torah), they were nevertheless baffled by Jesus' actions toward others. Especially offensive was his exuberant response to repentant "sinners" and his practice of "wining and dining" with them (Matt. 11:19/Luke 7:34). Suspicions were quickly followed by criticism. Jesus responded with an outpouring of his most memorable stories.

If the parables in Part One were mostly spoken to sympathetic audiences in desperate need of the hope they engendered, the parables in this section were most likely all addressed, initially, to critics.

Three of these parables are grouped together by Luke and touch upon a common theme: compassion for "sinners."

(b) Getting acquainted with the texts

The texts of the parable of the Lost Sheep provide an especially graphic example of the way a parable spoken by Jesus to one situation was adapted by the early church for another. For this reason we have already looked at it in our discussion (in the Introduction) on "Why differing versions of the same parable?" I will not repeat here all that was said there about the differences and similarities between the Matthew and Luke versions of this text. Instead I will simply take note of the fact that, in addition to the two canonical versions of this parable, we now have a third one available for study, the one in Thomas, and comment briefly on all three.

Let's begin by looking at the three texts side by side:

Matthew 18:12–14	Luke 15:4–7	Thomas 107
What do you think? If a man has a hundred sheep, and one of them has gone astray, does he not leave the ninety-nine on the hills and go in search of the one that went astray? And if he finds it, truly, I say to you, he rejoices over it more than over the ninety-nine that never went astray.	What man of you, having a hundred sheep, if he has lost one of them, does not leave the ninety-nine in the wilderness, and go after the one which is lost, until he finds it? And when he has found it, he lays it on his shoulders, rejoicing. And when he comes home, he calls his neighbors, saying to them, "Rejoice with me for I have found my	The Kingdom is like a shepherd who had a hundred sheep. One of them, the biggest, went astray. He left the ninety-nine and sought after the one till he found it. When he had laboured, he said to the sheep: I love thee more than the ninety-nine.

So it is not the will of my Father who is in heaven that one of these little ones should perish.

sheep which was lost." Just so, I tell you, there will be more joy in heaven over one sinner who repents than over ninety-nine righteous persons who need no repentance.

In comparing and analyzing Matthew's and Luke's versions of this text (again, see our discussion in the Introduction), it becomes evident that the differences are due to differing settings in which and for which the parable was told in each case. Luke informs us that the parable's original setting was a time when the Pharisees were criticizing Jesus because "this man receives sinners and eats with them" (Luke 15:2). The parable in Luke was thus clearly understood to be a response to this charge. The sheep (according to Luke) was "lost" (not just straying as in Matthew), and the shepherd seeks it "until he finds it." He is so joyful when he does that he summons his friends to a celebration (this part is missing in Matthew). The conclusion of Luke's parable is that just as the shepherd rejoices over the lost sheep that is found so there is joy in heaven over every "sinner" who repents.

According to Matthew this parable was spoken to disciples (Matt. 18:1) and had to do not with Jewish "sinners" but "straying" church members (Matt. 18:15–17). It concludes by stressing that "it is not the *will* of my Father who is in heaven that one of these little ones should perish." Therefore if a "brother sins" (goes astray) one should not just forget about him, but go after him and try to win him back (Matt. 18:15). Certainly this is an appropriate didactic extension of the parable's meaning, even though Luke has probably preserved the more original point and context with his emphasis on the shepherd's *joy* over the lost sheep when it was found ("heaven's" joy over repentant sinners).

The Thomas version illustrates what can happen when a parable is reapplied without any thought as to its original meaning. In Thomas the sheep that went astray "was the biggest." Thus the motive for seeking it lies in the superior value of this particular sheep. This sheep is so valuable in fact that the shepherd exclaims upon finding it that he loves it "more than the ninety-nine." What is celebrated in the parable, as Thomas tells it, is not the compassion and love of God for those who go astray (Matthew), or get lost in "sin" (Luke), but the far greater value of the sheep that was lost over all others. Obviously this sheep symbolized for the community that edited the Gospel of Thomas its own special and (to them) supremely valuable teachings. Whereas Jesus told the story of the Lost Sheep to awaken compassion for "sinners," it was retold by the Thomas Christians to awaken respect for their own rather esoteric knowledge (gnosis)! Parables students beware!

(c) Deciding which text to study

It should be clear from what is said above (as well as from our discussion of these texts in the Introduction) that Luke's version is the more original. Matthew's version reflects a growing preoccupation with church discipline among the early Christians, whereas Luke's version relates to a controversy over Jesus' association with sinners that was very soon at the center of his public mission.

(c) Meaning in the setting of Jesus' life

There is nothing that Jesus did that offended his contemporaries more than his practice of "receiving sinners and eating with them" (Luke 15:2). In that day to "eat" with someone was an act of communion. That Jesus ate with "sinners" could mean only one thing: he must be one of them. "Behold, a glutton and a drunkard, a friend of tax collectors and sinners" (Matt. 11:19; Luke 7:34). But who, more specifically, were these "sinners"?

"In the world of Jesus, the term 'sinner' had a quite definite ring. It was not only a fairly general designation for those who notoriously failed to observe the commandments of God and at whom, therefore, everyone pointed a finger, but also a specific term for those engaged in despised trades" (Joachim Jeremias, *N. T. Theology*).

To associate with such people, it was thought, inevitably led to compromise and tainting of the purity of those who wanted to do right. For this reason the Jewish leaders advocated a strict policy of "apartness." This in fact is what the word Pharisee means: "separation." "The supreme religious duty for contemporary Judaism, was

to keep away from sinners" (Jeremias). It was forbidden for a Pharisee to entertain a "sinner" as guest in his home or to show mercy
to those who were without "knowledge" of the law.

It is not difficult to see how the parable of the Lost Sheep relates
to this tragic situation. It is framed as a question: "What man of you
. . . ?" What man of you having a flock of 100 sheep, and suddenly
realizing that one of them is missing, would not leave the 99 in the
wilderness and go searching for it? The answer implied is: "No one!"
That is precisely the way a shepherd would act under the circumstances! When a shepherd loses a sheep, he risks everything to find
it. And when he does, what a joy he feels as he swings the sheep over
his shoulders and returns home!

That, Jesus says (interpreting in this instance his own parable),
is the way "heaven" feels about a "sinner" who repents. In fact
"there is more joy in heaven over one sinner who repents than over
ninety-nine righteous persons who need no repentance." There is a
barb in this climactic word. The ninety-nine righteous *think* they
need no repentance. That of course is the critical flaw in Pharisaism
to which Jesus returns again and again.

Through this parable, then, Jesus is defending himself against
false accusations. If he associates with sinners, it is by no means because he shares their moral outlook. It is because he believes God
is compassionate toward those who lose their way, and joyful when
they find it again. He is only acting (he says, in effect) in harmony
with "heaven."

Again we will postpone the discussion of the relevance of this
and the following two parables until we have had a chance to look
at all three.

10. THE LOST COIN (Luke 15:8–10)

(a) Getting oriented

There are many so-called "twin parables" in the Gospels. "Twin
parables" are two closely related stories that have been grouped together. In most instances this pairing of stories is secondary. The early church or the Gospel editors themselves have arranged them this

way. It is very possible, however, that the twin parables of the Lost Sheep and the Lost Coin were originally told on the same occasion. If so, they complement each other in an interesting way. The central figure of the one is a man; of the other a woman. The shepherd is moderately wealthy; the woman is obviously poor. Both, however, are alike in their joy in finding something they lost.

(b) Getting acquainted with the text

Since only Luke in this instance has preserved the text of this parable, we must rely completely on his version. There is no reason to doubt he has preserved it accurately. It reads as follows:

> Or what woman, having ten silver coins, if she loses one coin, does not light a lamp and sweep the house and seek diligently until she finds it?
>
> And when she has found it, she calls together her friends and neighbors, saying, "Rejoice with me, for I have found the coin which I have lost."
>
> Just so, I tell you, there is joy before the angels of God over one sinner who repents.

This parable, like the previous one, is narrated in the form of a question. "Tell me, what woman under these circumstances would not act precisely this way?"

The ten silver coins referred to may be the woman's wedding dowry that she wears around her neck. They are worth several dollars apiece. That she has only ten of them suggests that she brought with her into her marriage a very small dowry indeed. "Today many a woman prides herself on a head-dress of hundreds of gold and silver coins" (Jeremias). Besides, she lives in a miserable house without windows and a very low door. As a result she has to light a lamp in order to search for the lost coin.

Can you imagine a woman under these circumstances simply ignoring the loss of one of her precious coins? By no means! Rather she will take a palm twig (Jeremias) and sweep and sweep until she finds it. And then what joy! Just see her as she goes running from friend to friend, telling the glad news!

(c) Deciding which text to study

Fortunately in a few cases we can dispense with problems involved in explaining and choosing between several texts and proceed at once to the study of the text we have. This is such a case.

(d) Meaning in the setting of Jesus' life

Jesus is again speaking to his critics (Luke 15:1f.), to those who are offended by his easy manner in relating to "sinners." He does not minimize the fact that these "sinners" really are lost. But why for that reason ostracize them? Doesn't a shepherd when losing a sheep seek it until he finds it? Doesn't a poor woman who loses a coin turn her house upside down to find it? And what joy when they do! Likewise, there is tremendous joy in heaven over even one sinner who repents. "This is why I am entertaining them," Jesus implies. Something very wonderful is going on among these disaffiliated, alienated ones, something worth celebrating. They are being found by God again.

11. THE LOST SON (Luke 15:11–32)

(a) Getting oriented

The lost sheep and the lost coin are clearly symbolic. It is not lost sheep or coins that Jesus is talking about, but lost people. His critics were pointing a finger at him for "receiving sinners and eating with them."

The parable of the Lost Son moves a dramatic step closer to the reality being symbolized. The "Lost Son" is no mere symbol, but himself a flagrant example of precisely what the word "sinner" must have meant in that time.

(b) Getting acquainted with the text

Fortunately in getting acquainted with this matchless story we are spared the necessity of working our way through a lot of textual problems. Only Luke records it and in such a way that no one has doubted its essential accuracy.

There was a man who had two sons; and the younger of them said to his father, "Father, give me the share of property that falls to me."

And he divided his living between them.

Not many days later, the younger son gathered all he had and took his journey into a far country, and there he squandered his property in loose living. So he went and joined himself to one of the citizens of that country, who sent him into the fields to feed swine. And he would gladly have fed on the pods that the swine ate; and no one gave him anything.

But when he came to himself he said, "How many of my father's hired servants have bread enough and to spare, but I perish here with hunger! I will arise and go to my father, and I will say to him, 'Father, I have sinned against heaven and before you; I am no longer worthy to be called your son; treat me as one of your hired servants.' "

And he arose and came to his father.

But while he was yet at a distance, his father saw him and had compassion, and ran and embraced him and kissed him.

And the son said to him, "Father, I have sinned against heaven and before you; I am no longer worthy to be called your son."

But the father said to his servants, "Bring quickly the best robe, and put it on him; and put a ring on his hand, and shoes on his feet; and bring the fatted calf and kill it, and let us eat and make merry; for this my son was dead, and is alive again; he was lost, and is found."

And they began to make merry.

Now his elder son was in the field; and as he came and drew near to the house, he heard music and dancing. And he called one of the servants and asked what this meant. And he said to him, "Your brother has come, and your fa-

ther has killed the fatted calf, because he has received him
safe and sound."

But he was angry and refused to go in.

His father came out and entreated him, but he answered his father "Lo, these many years I have served you,
and I never disobeyed your command; yet you never gave
me a kid, that I might make merry with my friends. But
when this son of yours came, who has devoured your living
with harlots, you killed for him the fatted calf!"

And he said to him, "Son, you are always with me,
and all that is mine is yours. It was fitting to make merry
and be glad, for this brother was dead, and is alive; he was
lost, and is found."

Traditionally this has been called the parable of the Prodigal Son.
The parable itself, however, begins by stressing that there were "*two*
sons," not just one, and it is the obedient elder one, not the younger
prodigal, who is center stage in the parable's final climactic scene.
Jesus told another story with this same theme (Matt. 21:28–32).

It is the younger son, however, who sets the story in motion by
approaching his father for his share of the inheritance. Not much is
made of this in the story, but the original audience would know right
off that this boy is "no good." He does not care about his father's
welfare. He just wants to get his money and go.

He is looking for adventure and soon finds it. The recently gotten inheritance is quickly dissipated in "loose living." The portrait
is realistic. It does not glamorize the conduct of this "prodigal son."
He suffers the worst fate imaginable for a Jewish young man: feeding
pigs, friendless and desperately hungry. In the latter part of the story
the father twice exclaims: My son was dead . . . lost. This is what it
meant for a Jewish boy to be dead and lost.

But then he "came to himself." The scene is psychologically
true to life. His motives at first are rather shallow. He remembers
how well off he was at home, and decides it would be better to admit
his mistake and return as a "hired servant" than to continue his present way of life. He heads home in a somewhat fearful and legalistic
frame of mind.

Unlike the parables of the Lost Coin and the Lost Sheep, no one goes out seeking this Lost Son. But we do learn that the father has had him very much in mind, for "while he was yet at a distance," he saw him and ran to greet him. He was watching for his return. That the father "ran" is out of character for a dignified Palestinian householder (Jeremias)! Certainly too the way he treats the son is extravagant, to say the least. He scarcely hears the son's confession before he is shouting command after command to his servants. The son is fully reinstated as a member of the household (kiss, ring, robe, sandals) and preparations are immediately set in motion for a great feast. The contrast between the son's previous poverty and this reception is as sharply drawn as possible. The son has come home. This is what it meant in that day to be "alive" and "found."

But the story does not end there. This is one of Jesus' two-part stories, and all that was said to this point is only a backdrop, so to speak, for what now follows. The elder brother, about whom we have heard practically nothing so far, suddenly comes on stage. We learn at once what kind of person he is when we are told that he "was in the field." He is hardworking and responsible. And we can understand his reaction when he learns that a party with "music and dancing" is in progress for his younger brother, whose shameful conduct abroad was apparently known to him. His anger has a point. In responding to it, the father does not rebuke him but only repeats what he already told the servants. Something extraordinary has taken place that legitimately upsets the necessary routines of life and makes it "fitting to make merry and be glad." A "brother" that was dead is living again, a son that was lost is found.

(c) Deciding which text to study

Again we can dispense with this step, having only one text, and this an unquestioned masterpiece of the story-telling art of Jesus.

(d) Meaning in the setting of Jesus' life

If in the younger son Jesus portrayed a typical Jewish "sinner," in the elder brother he has captured exactly the attitude of the Pharisees. This latter portrait is by no means an unsympathetic one. The elder son's obedience and steady service are gratefully acknowledged: "Son, you are always with me . . ." There is not the slightest question but that he is morally superior to his younger brother in almost every respect.

But yet there is a defect. It is only hinted at, except for one sentence: "But while he was yet at a distance, his father saw him and had compassion . . ." What distinguishes the attitude of the father toward his profligate son from that of the elder brother is that the father had compassion. The Pharisees were virtuous men, but they lacked compassion.

Matthew quotes Jesus as having said: "Unless your righteousness exceeds that of the scribes and Pharisees, you will never enter the kingdom of heaven" (Matt. 5:20). Perhaps in no other story has Jesus succeeded so well in conveying what he meant by that goodness which goes beyond the noble virtues of these otherwise excellent men.

Through this parable Jesus challenges these Pharisees to do some self-reflecting. Is their attitude toward "sinners" who are groping for a way back "home" a true reflection of the mind of God (whom they so zealously want to serve)? If a shepherd rejoices in finding a lost sheep, a poor woman in finding lost coins, and a father in seeing a lost son, how much more does heaven rejoice in every new beginning!

(e) Listening to the parable today

What do you hear as you retell these three parables we have just studied? I am reminded of a statement by Adolf Holl in his controversial book *Jesus in Bad Company*: " . . . His concern is always with the person for whom at any given moment things go badly."

Our age too is frightfully marked by "lost sheep," "lost coins," "lost sons and daughters."

As perhaps never before, children are leaving home prematurely and wandering about the world. Lacking the wisdom of experience and refusing to be guided by others, they only too often waste their substance in loose living. *In the complexity and freedom of modern life adolescence has become as turbulent a passage into adulthood as at any time in human history.*

How easy it is for those who escape this folly to fall into the attitude of the elder brother. How easy to turn to our "farming," to our work, and isolate ourselves from these wayward children. How easy to ridicule and judge them for their sinful ways. And even when they take a few tentative steps out of the "mess" in which they often find themselves, how easy to greet them with suspicion instead of compassion.

How will these lost ones ever be found? How will these dead ones ever come alive? Only (Jesus seems to be saying) through compassionate love reaching out to small "turnings." Only through a risky readiness to embrace before the repentance has quite arrived. Only by "throwing parties" for those who are not yet quite worthy of them.

QUESTIONS FOR DISCUSSION AND FURTHER STUDY:

1. Who is "lost" in your neighborhood?
2. How do you feel toward them?
3. What are you doing to help them?

V. GENEROSITY

12. THE GENEROUS EMPLOYER (Matt. 20:1–16)

(a) Getting oriented

The next three parables are closely related to the ones we have just studied. Something is amiss, they suggest, in the outlook of those who profess to set the standards of "righteousness." Their attitude toward "sinners" is cold and distant. They lack compassion. But even more they lack generosity, and this because they do not understand that generosity (not justice) is at the heart of the universe.

(b) Getting acquainted with the text

Only Matthew has incorporated this parable into his Gospel. The text is excellent. The context, however, has given rise to some misconceptions. As it now stands, the parable is framed by a short saying: "But many that are first will be last, and the last first" (Matt. 19:30); "so the last will be first, and the first last" (Matt. 20:16). This saying is a promise and a warning. It suggests that many who are first now will be last later (on the day of judgment), and those last now will be first later on. Specifically it holds out a promise to disciples who are being persecuted (Matt. 19:28f.). One day they shall be rewarded.

The editor of Matthew's Gospel must have put this parable in this context because he thought it was related somehow to this idea. It too, he must have thought, speaks of a reversal of fortunes on the day of judgment. Perhaps he was thinking of that point in the parable where the vineyard owner says to his steward, "Call the laborers and pay them their wages, beginning with the last, up to the first." But this is hardly a reversal of fortunes, for as it turns out in the end *all* the laborers receive the same wage.

Viewed apart from its present context, the parable will readily be seen to have another focus. *As we read it, we should keep our eye not on the fate of the workers but on the rather peculiar behavior of the householder.*

> For the kingdom of heaven is like a householder [landowner] who went out early in the morning to hire laborers for his vineyard.
>
> After agreeing with the laborers for a denarius a day, he sent them into his vineyard.
>
> And going out about the third hour he saw others standing idle in the market place; and to them he said, "You go into the vineyard too, and whatever is right I will give you."
>
> So they went.
>
> Going out again about the sixth hour and the ninth hour he did the same.
>
> And about the eleventh hour he went out and found others standing; and he said to them, "Why do you stand here idle all day?" They said to him, "Because no one has hired us." He said to them, "You go into the vineyard too."
>
> And when evening came, the owner of the vineyard said to his steward, "Call the laborers and pay them their wages, beginning with the last, up to the first."
>
> And when those hired about the eleventh hour came, each of them received a denarius.
>
> Now when the first came, they thought they would receive more; but each of them also received a denarius.
>
> And on receiving it they grumbled at the householder,

saying, "These last worked only one hour, and you have made them equal to us who have borne the burden of the day and the scorching heat."

But he replied to one of them, "Friend, I am doing you no wrong; did you not agree with me for a denarius? Take what belongs to you, and go; I choose to give to this last as I give to you. Am I not allowed to do what I choose with what belongs to me? Or do you begrudge my generosity?"

One must admit that this vineyard owner has not planned his day very well. He hires one group of men, then a few hours later another, and so on until just one hour before quitting time. This rather odd behavior would certainly arouse the curiosity of the parable's original audience. What's going on here?

A hint as to where the story is heading is dropped when those hired first are promised that they will receive for their work the going rate of "a denarius a day," and those hired later on "whatever is right." Suddenly then we are transported to the end of the day when the laborers are paid, "beginning with the last up to the first." That in itself has no significance, except that, for the sake of the final scene, the story has to be told in such a way that those who worked longest will find out how those fared who came to work last. And what is it that then happens? The vineyard owner pays them all the same wage!

At this point the story shifts into high gear. This is another of Jesus' two-part parables, which always seem to speed up in the second part. Here is where their thrust lies. In this instance a rather tense dialogue explodes between the twelve-hour workers and the vineyard owner. "How can you be so unfair?" they say in effect. "We worked the entire day, through all the drudgery and heat of it, and have no more wages to show for our labors than these who worked only one hour."

The reply of the vineyard owner is devastating: "Friend," he says (and by friend is meant, not "buddy," but "sir"), "I've paid you what I promised. Take it and go. Am I not allowed to do what I want with what belongs to me? Or do you resent my generosity?"

This final sentence is surely crucial. Literally the Greek reads: "Or is your eye evil because I am good."

The parable itself has nothing to do with "reversal of fortunes." It says nothing about the "first being last and the last being first." Those who came to work at the beginning of the day received the agreed-upon wage. Those who came later on receive more than they might normally expect. The vineyard owner has been both fair and generous. All have received justice; some have been treated generously.

(c) Deciding which text to study

For reasons that should be clear from what has already been said, this parable should be studied apart from its present context in Matthew's Gospel and without the attached saying: "So the last will be first and the first last" (Matt. 20:16).

(d) Meaning in the setting of Jesus' life

Without a doubt the Pharisees are once again the target of this parable. We recognize at once in these hardworking vineyard laborers, who doggedly bear the burden and heat of the day, the figure of the "elder brother." What is it about these men that makes them so hostile toward those who do not work as hard as they do?

The answer is sharply etched in the words put into their mouths: ". . . you have made them equal to us who have borne the burden and heat of the day." They are motivated by a profound sense of "fairness." They want to see an exact correspondence between work and wages.

Jesus does not challenge this sense of fairness. It is correct as far as it goes. "Take what belongs to you, and go." But it does not go far enough. There are other dynamics at work in this world.

The Pharisees are disciplined and good, but their goodness is spoiled by their lack of generosity.

Again we will postpone the discussion of the relevance of this parable for today until we have looked at the next two parables in this group.

13. THE GOOD SAMARITAN (Luke 10:29-37)

(a) Getting oriented

In the background of the parables we have looked at so far in this section of our study (beginning with the parable of the Lost Sheep) is the harsh attitude of the Pharisees toward "sinners." But the mental outlook that made these "good" people so aloof toward "sinners" also distorted their relations with other Palestinian groups—the Samaritans for example.

(b) Getting acquainted with the text

Only Luke has recorded this well-known story. Its setting in his Gospel, however, is similar to a situation also described in Matthew (22:34–40) and Mark (12:28–31). As they tell it, Jesus was approached by a Pharisaic lawyer ("scribe" in Mark) and asked what he thought was the "first" (Mark) or "great" (Matt.) commandment. In Luke the lawyer wonders what he must "do to inherit eternal life." Jesus asks him to answer his own question on the basis of his knowledge of the law. In all three Gospels the double commandment of love for God and neighbor is cited as the answer.

At this point Luke records a follow-up conversation between the lawyer and Jesus, and then the parable of the Good Samaritan. Why is this missing in the other Gospels? Is this setting of the parable original or one that Luke himself (or his tradition) constructed? According to Luke the parable was told in response to the question: Who is my neighbor? This is *not,* however, the question posed at the conclusion of the parable itself.

The parable of the Good Samaritan is so familiar that we will have to read it with special care if we are to hear it afresh. Let's look at it, first of all, apart from its editorial framework.

A man was going down from Jerusalem to Jericho, and he fell among robbers, who stripped him and beat him, and departed, leaving him half dead.

Now by chance a priest was going down that road; and when he saw him, he passed by on the other side.

So likewise a Levite, when he came to the place and saw him, passed by on the other side.

But a Samaritan, as he journeyed, came to where he was; and when he saw him, he had compassion, and went to him and bound up his wounds, pouring on oil and wine; then he set him on his own beast and brought him to an inn, and took care of him. And the next day he took out two denarii and gave them to the innkeeper, saying, "Take care of him; and whatever more you spend, I will repay you when I come back." Which of these three, do you think, proved neighbor to the man who fell among the robbers?

The final question is crucial for interpreting this parable: "Which of these three . . . proved neighbor . . . ?" Not: Who is my neighbor but, *which of the three examples cited was* a neighbor? It might seem that the answer is simple, but there are certain subtleties to this parable that can only be appreciated as we understand something about each of the people described.

There is first of all the "man" who fell among robbers. About him, apart from describing the way he was attacked and its consequences, we are told nothing. He is not a central figure. He is just a man—a human being.

The next two people mentioned are personnel of the Jerusalem temple, possibly on their way to or from their tour of duty there. As such they are symbols of the religious elite from whom one might expect praiseworthy conduct. It is slightly jarring therefore when in both instances it is emphasized that even though they saw the half-dead man, they "passed by on the other side." Perhaps they were afraid of contaminating themselves through contact with a corpse, thus making themselves unfit for temple duty for a week (Num. 19:11–12).

And now one expects that a third person will go by, and it will surely be a Jewish layman, perhaps one of the "people of the land" (the common people).

When instead Jesus said: "But a Samaritan . . ." the story's rhythm is rudely upset. Priest, Levite, layman—yes. That makes sense. But Priest, Levite, Samaritan? That is a semantic shock (Crossan). It is like saying: Minister, deacon, Communist, or bishop, priest, Buddhist!

That the story at this point turns a corner is also indicated by the way the description suddenly expands. It is not enough to say that this Samaritan helped the poor dying man. No, we are told step by step what he did, beginning from the moment he saw him and "had compassion," to his final instructions to the innkeeper "to take care of him." Twenty-six words are used to describe the fate of the man who fell among robbers; twenty-two to tell of the priest; nineteen of the Levite; but no less than eighty-five words are used to describe the Samaritan and his actions (Crossan)! Rightly is this parable called the parable of the Good Samaritan. That is where it concentrates.

But the fact that we speak today of the "Good" Samaritan resolves too quickly the very tension that the story itself was originally designed to create. For the last person in the world the Jews of that time would have called "good" was a Samaritan.

We cannot understand this parable unless we recall that in the time of Jesus Jews and Samaritans were at bitter odds with one another. "For Jews have no dealings with Samaritans" (John 4:9). That puts it mildly. They hated one another with a hatred that was centuries old. "There are two nations that my soul detests," writes the urbane and usually level-headed Jesus ben Sirach (whose book of wise sayings is a part of the Apocrypha), "the third is not a nation at all: the inhabitants of Mount Seir, and the Philistines, and the stupid people living at Shechem [the Samaritans]" (Ecclus. 50:27–29).

The question at the end of this parable, then, is an explosive one: "*Which of these three* do you think proved neighbor ... ?" If this question was put to a Pharisaic lawyer (as Luke indicates), he was certainly put to the test by it.

Which of these three? Can you say it? The *Samaritan!* No, the lawyer cannot say it. He avoids the despised name, but he must admit it was the "one who showed mercy" (Luke 10:37).

(c) Deciding which text to study

The tension between the lawyer's question ("And who is my neighbor?") and the climactic question of the parable itself ("Which of these three, do you think, proved neighbor . . . ?") suggests that the setting of this parable may be secondary—a creation of Luke or his tradition. In order to catch the full impact of the parable in its original setting, it should be studied, initially at least, apart from its familiar editorial framework.

(d) Meaning in the setting of Jesus' life

Like the parable of the Lost Son, this story is so close to the reality being talked about that it verges on being an example rather than a parable. The Samaritan is model (not just symbol) of the attitudes Jesus wants to awaken. "Go and do likewise" (Luke 10:37).

But as we have just seen the story is not as simple and straightforward as at first it might appear. More is at stake than "Be kind to the next person who needs you." By choosing the Samaritan as the model of generous, compassionate behavior, Jesus forces his Pharisaic audience to reconsider not only its attitude toward the man fallen among thieves but also to the man in the story who helped him. The question posed is not only how generous are we toward those who need help, but what about our attitude toward those we despise as spiritually inferior to ourselves? The Pharisees were looking down not only on "sinners" but upon their Samaritan neighbors. Jesus' parable cuts away at this self-righteous posture.

Goodness, he seems to be saying, is goodness wherever it appears, and it appears in very unexpected places, sometimes among very negatively valued people.

14. THE LAST JUDGMENT (Matt. 25:31–46)

(a) Getting oriented

How deeply Jesus valued "generosity" receives its ultimate statement in the parable of the Last Judgment.

(b) Getting acquainted with the text

Frank Beare calls this story (which only Matthew has recorded) a "prophetic vision" rather than a "true parable." In any case its general features are "of such striking originality that it is difficult to credit them to anyone but the Master himself" (Manson, Jeremias).

The scene portrayed is that of the final judgment. Many elements in that scene are traditional, as we shall see.

Matthew's text reads as follows:

When the Son of man comes in his glory, and all the angels with him, then he will sit on his glorious throne. *Before him will be gathered all the nations,* and he will separate them one from another as a shepherd separates the sheep from the goats, and he will place the sheep at his right hand, but the goats at the left.

Then the King will say to those at his right hand, "Come, O blessed of my Father, inherit the kingdom prepared for you from the foundation of the world; for I was hungry and you gave me food, I was thirsty and you gave me drink, I was a stranger and you welcomed me, I was naked and you clothed me, I was sick and you visited me, I was in prison and you came to me."

Then the righteous will answer him, "Lord, when did we see thee hungry and feed thee, or thirsty and give thee drink? And when did we see thee a stranger and welcome thee, or naked and clothe thee? And when did we see thee sick or in prison and visit thee?"

And the King will answer them, "Truly, I say to you, as you did it to one of the least of these my brethren, you did it to me."

Then he will say to those at his left hand, "Depart from me, you cursed, into the eternal fire prepared for the devil and his angels; for I was hungry and you gave me no food, I was thirsty and you gave me no drink, I was a stranger and you did not welcome me, naked and you did not clothe me, sick and in prison and you did not visit me."

Then they also will answer, "Lord, when did we see

thee hungry or thirsty or a stranger or naked or sick or in prison, and did not minister to thee?"

Then he will answer them, "Truly, I say to you, as you did it not to one of the least of these, you did it not to me." And they will go away into eternal punishment, but the righteous into eternal life.

What is portrayed here is a judgment of the "nations." "Before him will be gathered all the nations . . ." The scene is drawn from Daniel 7, where Daniel saw a vision of "the ancient of days" taking his seat, and "one like a son of man" was given dominion over all peoples, nations and languages. This way of depicting the end of the age was very popular in Jesus' time.

But for the story that Jesus tells this is only background. It is not the ascendency of the son of man to power over the nations that is central here, but the surprising basis on which the nations are said to be judged. By far the greater part of the story is taken up with a dialogue between the son of man (the King) and those who have just received his verdict. *Everyone* is simply astonished at this verdict, both the righteous and the wicked. They had no idea that they were accepting or rejecting the King of the universe at the point where they helped or rejected the destitute. The fate of the nations, this story implies, will be hammered out on the anvil of generosity.

(c) Deciding which text to use

Matthew's text is the only one we have. For this reason it is difficult to know to what extent it might have been embellished. Uniquely Matthean terminology such as the opening reference to the son of man sitting on his glorious throne (cf. Matt. 19:28), "the righteous," "my brethren." "the eternal fire prepared for the devil and his angels" (cf. Matt. 13:40, 42, 50; 18:8) may be secondary. Experience in studying the parables to this point should also caution us against making too much of background details.

(d) Meaning in the setting of Jesus' life

It is especially important that we try to see this parable in the framework of Jesus' life. It is doubtful that its original purpose was to provide a literal, detailed picture of the day of judgment (as its context in Matthew's Gospel would suggest). Rather we would do well to interpret it (as we have the other parables) as originally conveying a rather focused message to a very specific audience. If we ask who that audience might have been, the controversy of Jesus with his Jewish contemporaries over what attitude to take toward "outsiders" again comes to mind. Like the other parables we have just studied, this one too seems to assault that wall of self-satisfaction that the Jewish religious elite had built around themselves. On judgment day there will be surprises right and left. What will count then is not self-conscious righteousness, but spontaneous generosity toward all who need it most. For what is done on behalf of the destitute is done to God. It is not the essential idea that is so novel here. Proverbs 14:31 and 17:5 say much the same thing. It is rather the way unpremeditated generosity is dramatized as decisive in the final judgment.

(e) Listening to the parable today

Another quote from *Jesus in Bad Company* by Adolf Holl seems to summarize my feelings as I listen to these parables. Writes Holl:

"What he might have brought about was the presence in societies touched by Christianity of men whose avowed purpose in life was goodness practised daily amidst the stink of misery and disease."

It is worth asking: why then has Christianity so often turned out so differently?

Holl provides a partial answer: Jesus has been progressively removed from the realm of ordinary men and made the object of veneration. *Instead of following him we worship him.*

Today this may be changing. Through historical study we are again coming face to face with the claims upon us of Jesus himself. His teachings once again stand before us in their stark simplicity.

But what will we do with them? The same motives that led to their being brushed aside in other times and places are at work today. We no less than those who have gone before us draw back from their disquieting challenge.

What is especially unnerving about these teachings is their lack of programmatic content. No one is immune from them or knows how to exhaust them in his living. If Jesus had said pay a tithe, we would know what to do to calm our conscience. If he had said join this or that church and fit into its system of charity, we could do it and then with our mind at ease go our conventional ways.

One point especially must come to mind for those of us in the West as we read these parables: the continuing stark imbalance in our world between the regions of wealth and the regions of poverty. So long as we meditate on parables of this kind we will never (in the West) be able to settle down into smug self-satisfaction. We can no longer hide behind the mantle of ignorance. We know what goes on in this world, and the challenge is ever before us to direct our energies to the amelioration of human suffering.

Not a single one of us can opt out of this obligation, for there is something that every last one of us can do.

It is frightfully easy in North American society, as it now exists, for white middle-class Americans to settle down into a pattern of sophisticated selfishness. Material needs abound, and emotional and spiritual needs arising from sin and folly as well. Compassion and generosity are required of us as never before, but not only for the sake of those in dire need, but as the *only* environment in which any one of us can genuinely live and grow and have our being.

QUESTIONS FOR DISCUSSION
AND FURTHER STUDY:

1. Are you generous? Why do you answer this question as you do?
2. Do you know anyone who is generous? Can you cite a contemporary "parable" of generosity?
3. What are you doing with your money? What proportion are you spending on yourself and your family? Are you as generous with others as you are with yourself?
4. What attitude do you take toward the problem of third-world poverty?

VI. HUMILITY

15. THE UNMERCIFUL SERVANT
(Matt. 18:23–35)

(a) Getting oriented

What is at the root of this coolness of the "righteous" toward the "sinner"? Why is it that human history disintegrates again and again into cold wars between persons, classes and nations? Why is there so little compassion and generosity?

The following parables may shed light on these questions. In any case they all touch on a pervasive human problem: pride. Where pride dominates, these stories suggest, the flow of compassion is stifled. Where humility reigns, generosity also will grow.

(b) Getting acquainted with the text

Again we have only one text of this parable, but it is a good one. Joachim Jeremias suggests one slight modification. In the final line the parable speaks of forgiving "your *brother*" from your heart. This might suggest Christian "brothers," and this in fact is how Matthew may have understood it. He has placed this parable at the end of a collection of sayings having to do with relationships in the "church" (Matt. 18:17). Originally Jesus would have meant forgiveness of "one another" (or anyone), not just of the brother in the church.

I suggest, then, that we read the parable as Matthew records it, but with one minor change in the last line:

> Therefore the kingdom of heaven may be compared to a king who wished to settle accounts with his servants.
>
> When he began the reckoning, one was brought to him who owed him ten thousand talents; and as he could not pay, his lord ordered him to be sold, with his wife and children and all that he had, and payment to be made.
>
> So the servant fell on his knees, imploring him, "Lord, have patience with me, and I will pay you everything."
>
> And out of pity for him the Lord of that servant released him and forgave him the debt.
>
> But that same servant, as he went out, came upon one of his fellow servants who owed him a hundred denarii; and seizing him by the throat he said, "Pay what you owe."
>
> So his fellow servant fell down and besought him, "Have patience with me, and I will pay you."
>
> He refused and went and put him in prison till he should pay the debt.
>
> When his fellow servants saw what had taken place, they were greatly distressed, and they went and reported to their lord all that had taken place.
>
> Then his lord summoned him and said to him, "You wicked servant! I forgave you all that debt because you besought me; and should not you have had mercy on your fellow servant, as I had mercy on you?"
>
> And in anger his lord delivered him to the torturers, till he should pay all his debt.
>
> So also my heavenly Father will do to every one of you, if you do not forgive your brother [one another] from your heart.

In Matthew this parable is immediately preceded by a dialogue between Jesus and Peter in which Peter asks: "Lord, how often shall my brother sin against me, and I forgive him?" Jesus replies: ". . . seventy times seven."

The parable of the Unmerciful Servant, however, is not about *how often* to forgive but about *failure to forgive at all,* and this on the part of someone who himself has been forgiven a great deal.

The setting of the story is the court of a potentate. This great king has delegated sections of his kingdom to "servants." As the story opens, he is holding court and his servants are being questioned as to how they have handled the affairs of their sector of the kingdom.

Right off the king is confronted by a servant who is hopelessly in debt. He has mismanaged his affairs to the tune of 10,000 talents. "The monstrous nature of this fantastic sum becomes apparent when it is remembered that the yearly tribute of Galilee and Perea in 4 B.C. amounted to 200 talents . . . a 50th of that sum" (Jeremias)! If the story were told today, we might say that this poor fellow owed a billion dollars.

The king is furious and orders him sold, along with his wife, children, and possessions.

The servant falls on his knees and begs for patience, *promising that he will pay everything,* an obviously ludicrous idea! How could he possibly pay off such an enormous debt? But wonder of wonders, the king is moved to pity and sends him away scot-free, the impossible debt totally canceled.

But now comes the crunch. Released from his debt of millions, the servant seizes a fellow servant for failure to pay a debt of a few thousand dollars and has him thrown in jail. Cries for mercy fall on deaf ears.

But the story is not finished. The king learns of what has happened and summons the hard-hearted servant before him for a scathing admonition, the punchline of which was: ". . . and should not you have had mercy on your fellow servant, as I had mercy on you?" Then "in anger" the king withdrew his forgiveness and had him thrown in jail.

The story closes with a warning: Be prepared for disaster if you're not prepared for mercy.

(c) Deciding which text to study

Matthew's version of this parable is excellent, although it is possible that the original parable may have ended with the king's admonition (realistically, would even a king dare withdraw a pardon?). If so, the closing warning ("so also my heavenly Father will do to every one of you, if . . .") is editorial as well. Jesus usually lets his stories speak for themselves.

(d) Meaning in the setting of Jesus' life

Many of Jesus' parables have a touch of humor. The humor is especially apparent in this one. It is really laughable how this servant behaves. First of all he promises to pay a hopelessly large debt, if only given enough time. And then, when forgiven millions of dollars, he turns and refuses to forgive a man who owes him a few thousand dollars. This man is really pathetic.

There is little doubt that in the background, once again, is the piety of the Pharisees. "In Pharisaic Judaism, sin is made innocuous by two things: by casuistry and by the idea of merit" (Joachim Jeremias, *N. T. Theology,* p. 147). Casuistry sees sin in terms of specific cases. There are 613 laws in the Jewish scriptures. The main thing is to obey them and accumulate merit "in heaven." The more obedience the larger will grow the heavenly bank account, and one can then stop worrying about sinful debts.

The result of this type of thinking is twofold: One begins to imagine that he can "pay everything"; one becomes hard on others who do not pay up. In short, such people become cruel because they forget how much they too are "sinners" in need of forgiveness.

Pharisaic snobbishness and lack of compassion spring from lack of humility. "You would not find it so hard to forgive were you to understand how much you have been forgiven." If the final scene is authentic, there is also a warning in this parable: "your pettiness will be found out, and then you will suffer for it."

Again we will wait until we have looked at all the parables of this group before exploring their relevance for today.

16. THE PHARISEE AND THE TAX COLLECTOR
(Luke 18:9–14)

(a) Getting oriented

Many of the parables describe the Pharisees (as we have seen), but in a subtle "metaphorical" manner. Their virtues and vices, as Jesus saw them, are only hinted at in the elder brother, the complaining vineyard workers (who sweated through the heat of the day), and the unmerciful servant. In the story to which we now turn symbolism is dropped. A Pharisee himself comes on stage as a Pharisee.

(b) Getting acquainted with the text

Only Luke has the text of this parable. He introduces it with the following words: "He [Jesus] also told this parable to some who trusted in themselves that they were righteous and despised others" (Luke 18:9). This is the way Luke understood it, and there is no reason in this instance to disagree with him. However, we should let the parable speak for itself.

This advice applies as well to the saying that is appended to the parable: "for everyone who exalts himself will be humbled, but he who humbles himself will be exalted" (Luke 9:14). This is an independent saying that appears elsewhere in the Gospels (Matt. 23:12; Luke 14:11). It is not quite to the point of this parable and should be left to one side as the parable itself is studied.

Two men went up into the temple to pray, one a Pharisee and the other a tax collector.

The Pharisee stood and prayed thus with himself, "God, I thank thee that I am not like other men, extortioners, unjust, adulterers, or even like this tax collector.

I fast twice a week, I give tithes of all that I get."

But the tax collector, standing far off, would not even lift up his eyes to heaven, but beat his breast, saying, "God, be merciful to me a sinner!"

I tell you, this man went down to his house justified rather than the other.

It would have shocked Jesus' original audience to hear a Pharisee and a tax collector compared in this way. The one was a "national hero," the other a "national disgrace" (Flood). The Pharisees were the backbone of Jewish identity at a time when that identity was close to being lost. The tax collectors were enemy collaborators. The Pharisees did their very best to obey God's commandments. The tax collectors were "robbers and thieves." They had no civil rights and were shunned by all who wanted to live respectable lives.

It was certainly a surprise, then, to the original audience when Jesus said: "I tell you, this man [the tax collector] went down to his house justified rather than the other." Why? The reason is not all that apparent.

Take the prayer of the Pharisee. What is really wrong with it? He is grateful to God for having been spared a life of sin. "There but for the grace of God go I." In the Jewish Talmud, interestingly enough, there appears a prayer that is remarkably similar to this one:

> I thank thee, O Lord, my God, that thou hast given me my lot with those who sit in the house of learning, and not with those who sit at the street-corners; for I am early to work, and they are early to work; I am early to work on the words of the Torah, and they are early to work on things of no moment. I weary myself, and they weary themselves; I weary myself and profit thereby, and they weary themselves to no profit. I run, and they run; I run towards the life of the age to come, and they run towards the pit of destruction.

This suggests that the prayer of the Pharisee in Jesus' parable belongs to an established liturgical tradition in which gratitude is expressed for the privilege of living a life of obedience to Torah (law).

The tax collector, on the other hand, frankly admits that he is a disreputable "sinner." And while his prayer is touching, it might well be asked, what is he going to do about the mess he's gotten himself into? Will this wicked fellow really make restitution for all his past crimes and change his ways? That Jesus regards this tax collector as "justified" rather than the Pharisee, and this on the basis of a single prayer for mercy, arouses perplexity and a second look.

"I am not like other men . . ." says the Pharisee to himself. He is not only grateful for having been spared a life of sin, he actually thinks he has no sin at all. He is a man set apart from others. "I fast twice a week, I give tithes of all that I get." He is proud of some of the extra things he does. The law requires that a Jew fast one day a year. He fasts twice a week. The law (as then interpreted) does not require a tithe of certain agricultural items that were already tithed by the farmer who grew them. But this man makes no distinctions. He tithes everything. One feels that this Pharisee is not really talking to God so much as meditating to himself (and with eyes open to what is going on around him).

The tax collector on the other hand is in the grip of a strong emotion. He stands afar off, beats his breast, and cannot even bring himself to lift up his eyes to heaven. His prayer is short, more like a cry. He is trusting his whole life to the mercy of God.

(c) Deciding which text to study

The parable should be studied apart from Luke's introductory explanation (Luke 18:9) and the attached maxim (about the humble being exalted, and the proud being humbled). Although both are appropriate comments, they were not part of the original story.

(d) Meaning in the setting of Jesus' life

There is nothing romantic about these portraits. Jesus is not exalting the tax collector or downplaying the Pharisee. The tax collector was indeed a sinner, and the Pharisee had many virtues. But the Pharisees had an exaggerated idea of themselves. They thought they were a class apart. Their zeal for obeying the law made them inhuman.

This is something Jesus felt with a passion: virtue without humility is deadening; sin with contrition is full of hope. The humble prayer for mercy on the part of a criminal pleases God more than the self-righteous prayer of thanks on the part of the virtuous.

It is sobering to realize that Jesus' sharpest criticisms were directed not to those who were evil, but to those who were good— goodness, however, marred by pride and egotism.

17. THE TWO DEBTORS (Luke 7:41–43)

(a) Getting oriented

The very subtle way being "good" can distort one's attitude toward those who are "bad" is the theme of yet another parable: the parable of the Two Debtors.

(b) Getting acquainted with the text

The text of this parable is embedded in the account of an incident that took place during the visit of Jesus in the home of a Pharisee. In this instance there is no reason to doubt that this was the occasion when Jesus first told the story. It is an especially good example, therefore, of the very concrete situations to which many of the parables must have initially been addressed (see our discussion of this parable in the Introduction, p. 7):

> One of the Pharisees asked him to eat with him, and he went into the Pharisee's house, and sat at table.
>
> And behold, a woman of the city, who was a sinner, when she learned that he was sitting at table in the Pharisee's house, brought an alabaster flask of ointment, and standing behind him at his feet, weeping, she began to wet his feet with her tears, and wiped them with the hair of her head, and kissed his feet, and anointed them with the ointment.
>
> Now when the Pharisee who had invited him saw it, he said to himself, "If this man were a prophet, he would have known who and what sort of woman this is who is touching him, for she is a sinner."
>
> And Jesus answering said to him, "Simon, I have something to say to you."
>
> And he answered, "What is it, Teacher?"
>
> "A certain creditor had two debtors; one owed five hundred denarii, and the other fifty. When they could not pay, he forgave them both. Now which of them will love him more?"

Simon answered, "The one, I suppose, to whom he forgave more."

And he said to him, "You have judged rightly."

Then turning toward the woman he said to Simon, "Do you see this woman? I entered your house, you gave me no water for my feet, but she has wet my feet with her tears and wiped them with her hair. You gave me no kiss, but from the time I came in she has not ceased to kiss my feet. You did not anoint my head with oil, but she has anointed my feet with ointment. Therefore I tell you, her sins, which are many, are forgiven, for she loved much; but he who is forgiven little, loves little."

And he said to her, "Your sins are forgiven."

Then those who were at table with him, began to say among themselves, "Who is this, who even forgives sins?" And he said to the woman, "Your faith has saved you; go in peace."

Again we are in the presence of a Pharisee, and not just a storybook Pharisee either. He is friendly toward Jesus, for he has invited him to his house for a meal. Joachim Jeremias suggests that Jesus might have spoken at the synagogue just prior to this occasion. It was customary for synagogue leaders to invite honored guests home for a meal.

If that were the case, we can imagine that Jesus might have spoken that day in such a way that the heart of a woman "who was a sinner" was moved to repentance.

In any case, while Jesus reclined at the meal, "a woman of the city" entered. She had been searching for Jesus, and finding him at last, she stood weeping, her tears falling on his feet. Impulsively she took off her head-covering, unbound her hair, and began wiping and kissing his feet. Her gratitude for what she had received through Jesus earlier in the day is overflowing.

For such a scandalous act a married woman might be divorced. But this woman may have had no husband. She is called a "woman of the city, who was a sinner," which probably means that she was a prostitute.

The attitude of Simon the Pharisee is restrained. He watches in solemn silence and perplexity, his apparent expectation that Jesus might be a prophet slowly crumbling. But Jesus senses what is going on in his mind and tells a parable. Two men are in debt to the same creditor. One owes ten times more than the other. *Neither* can pay and both are forgiven. "Now which of them will love him more?" With these few words this woman's actions are suddenly placed in a new light and the Pharisaic host is gently put on the spot. The answer is only too obvious, but Jesus wants him to think it through and state publicly his conclusion.

(c) Deciding which text to study

Would that we had (as here) the occasion described on which each of the parables was first given! How much easier our task in interpreting them would be. We should make the best use of this rare opportunity by studying both text and context together.

(d) Meaning in the setting of Jesus' life

"You have judged rightly" Jesus exclaimed when Simon responded as he did.

We can see here that Jesus' parables were not intended to teach general truths, but to awaken insight on the spot by very specific people in very specific situations.

Simon the Pharisee could not understand why Jesus allowed himself to be "touched" by a woman who was a sinner. This, he thought, showed a lack of "prophetic" insight and moral discernment. It is a very concrete example of the kind of attitude Jesus encountered repeatedly on the part of the Jewish religious elite.

The parable gently shifts the field of vision. The Pharisaic host is told to think of *two* people in debt, and hopelessly so, for they both must be forgiven. Certainly this is a subtle reminder to Simon that he too is in debt. To be sure, the debt of the one is ten times greater than that of the other. Jesus does not for a moment deny that the woman at his feet is anything but a sinner who has incurred a great debt before God, or that Simon is a far more upright person than she. But just that fact also explains her bizarre behavior. Those who are forgiven much will sometimes love much. At the root of the

Pharisaic lack of love and compassion is failure to see that they too are sinners in need of repentance and forgiveness.

"Go in peace," Jesus says to the woman, "your faith has saved you." Jesus valued more than anything else "faith" that moves a person out of a rut into something new and better. He respected the Pharisees, but was pained by their self-righteous attitudes toward others weaker than themselves.

18. ON CHOOSING WHERE TO SIT AT A BANQUET (Luke 14:7–11)

(a) Getting oriented

The defects in Pharisaic "righteousness" showed up not only in the way they treated "sinners" but in the way they treated one another. Their lack of humility, for example, was also evident in their conduct at a certain meal (Luke 14:1).

(b) Getting acquainted with the text

On the surface this text sounds like sage advice on how to get the prominent places at a banquet (not necessarily a "marriage feast" as the RSV translators indicate).

> When you are invited by any one to a marriage feast [or banquet] do not sit down in a place of honor, lest a more eminent man than you be invited by him; and he who invited you both will come and say to you, "Give place to this man," and then you will begin with shame to take the lowest place. But when you are invited, go and sit in the lowest place, so that when your host comes he may say to you, "Friend, go up higher"; then you will be honored in the presence of all who sit at table with you. For everyone who exalts himself will be humbled, and he who humbles himself will be exalted.

Luke (who is the only one to have recorded these words) insists that there is more here than at first one might suppose. This teaching is "parabolic," he tells us, and was spoken on a very specific occasion:

> Now he told a parable to those who were invited, when he
> marked how they chose the places of honor . . .

These editorial suggestions might well be correct. The "sage advice" is couched in rhythmic phrases that betray an intensity of emotion. Profound issues seem to be at stake in the way these distinguished men scramble for places of honor: "Everyone who exalts himself will be humbled, and he who humbles himself will be exalted." This maxim, which as we have seen is somewhat artificially appended to the parable of the Pharisee and the Tax Collector, sums up exactly the thrust of this parable.

(c) Deciding which text to study

In this instance Luke's editorial introduction, the "parable" itself, and the concluding maxim should all be studied together.

(d) Meaning in the setting of Jesus' life

The setting as Luke describes it (14:1) was a meal in the home of a prominent Pharisee. There was much ado at this banquet about who sits where. These good people were trying to outdo one another for positions of honor. This "superiority complex" is very similar to that which Jesus saw earlier on the face of a Pharisee as a "sinner" bathed his feet with tears. He saw it too in the look of a Pharisee at prayer as he compared himself with a tax collector. Now here it is again in the pompous rituals of the rich as they gathered to wine and dine.

David Granskau may be right that Jesus' response is tinged with humor. A smile may have flickered on his lips as he warned them against taking the places of honor and making fools of themselves. It was after all a well-known tradition that those with the highest social standing arrive at banquets last and displace those who presumptuously take the forward seats. But when he finished his audience must have wondered: "Is he only chiding us for our etiquette? Or

does he speak of something deeper than that? Our fundamental outlook on life, perhaps?"

In the events of a dinner party Jesus saw, parabolically, the
spiritual qualities that make for life and death.

19. ON THE ATTITUDE OF A SLAVE
(Luke 17:7–10)

(a) Getting oriented

One more short "parable" seems to be aimed at exposing a too
lofty way of thinking on the part of the Pharisees.

(b) Getting acquainted with the text

The text seems a bit cluttered with its three distinct questions,
but we have no way of knowing whether this was the case originally,
since we have only Luke's version to go by.

> Will any of you, who has a servant plowing or keeping
> sheep, say to him when he has come in from the field,
> "Come at once and sit down at table."
>
> Will he not rather say to him, "Prepare supper for me,
> and gird yourself and serve me, till I eat and drink; and
> afterward you shall eat and drink"?
>
> Does he thank the servant because he did what was
> commanded?
>
> So you also, when you have done all that is command-
> ed you, say, "We are simply slaves: we have only done
> what was our duty."

In the above text I have made one minor change in the Revised
Standard Version. Instead of "we are worthless slaves" (RSV), one
can also translate, "We are just poor [miserable] slaves" (Jeremias).
The slaves are not useless. They are simply slaves, that's all.

A slave, of course, is completely at the service of his master. The opening question therefore calls for a negative answer. Will anyone invite his slave, when he comes in from the field, to sit down at table with him? Well, of course not! No one treats a slave that way. Nor does a master hesitate asking his slave to prepare and serve him supper, before the slave eats and drinks. And when the slave has done all this, he does not necessarily thank him for obeying his commands. It is just assumed that this is what a slave will do.

(c) Deciding which text to study

Lacking parallels, we are compelled to take the text as Luke has preserved it, with the slight modification suggested above in translating the final line.

(d) Meaning in the setting of Jesus' life

We should not make too much of this parable. This is not a general statement about our relationship to God. Jesus' favorite image for that is the love that flows between father and son. If he wagers in this instance another image (that of master-slave), then it must be because he wants to say something quite specific to a particular group of people.

At this point in our study we do not need to wonder who that group might be. Again it must be the Pharisees, with their highly developed theology of merit. By obeying "all that is commanded" they thought they were laying up merit in heaven. This made them secure and proud. This, Jesus says, is a really false way of thinking. Rather we are at our best when we go about our work modestly and without thought of rewards or punishments.

(e) Listening to the parables today

As I listen to this group of parables I have the impression that here Jesus is not simply defending himself; he is taking the offensive. He is not only trying to explain why he associates with "sinners"; he is critiquing the Pharisees. There is something wrong with these good and successful members of his society. And precisely because what is wrong is among this group and because it is so pervasive among them, it radiates everywhere. It is the crack in the foundation of Judaism that more than anything else could lead to catastrophe.

And what is it?

Kierkegaard in his devotional classic, *Purity of Heart Is to Will One Thing,* comes close to describing it when he writes of the "Egocentric Service of the Good." Outright evil rarely wins the day. We can easily recognize the sinner as prostitute, thief, murderer, or swindler. But the evil to which Jesus points in the parables we have just studied parades in the garments of goodness. It is proud, self-centered devotion to a righteous cause—in short "self-righteousness." It is being good as a way of advancing the self-striving ego.

Kierkegaard goes on to speak of this evil as "a powerful deception." It looks for all the world like "purity of heart," but it is as far from authentic goodness "as the high place is from the deep chasm." It is goodness corrupted by "heaven-storming pride."

What is so moving about Pope John XXIII's *Journal of a Soul* is the ample evidence there of his lifelong combat with precisely this problem. Who would have guessed that this most humble and most beloved of twentieth-century popes waged a relentless war against the "egocentric service of the good" within himself? "Self-love" he calls it.

> Self-love! What a problem it is, when one stops to think about it! Who has ever defined it? What philosopher has dealt with it? It is the most important problem we have to deal with, truly a matter of life and death, and who cares about it? Yet, as I have seen in my recent meditations, Jesus Christ in his noble teaching is constantly showing us how in practice we must oppose this mortal enemy who corrupts all our actions.

Another contemporary "saint," Dom Helder Camara of Brazil, has also written of the importance of this struggle against pride:

> I have the impression [he writes] that God knows the importance of humility for man. He knows our weaknesses, our pride, and as I put it, he purposely sets on our path each day four or five humiliations. If we do not compre-

hend them, if we do not accept them, it's a serious matter. But if we accept them, then we learn the generosity of God. For the small offerings we manage to give, we always receive, during the rest of our life, grace after grace after grace. Perhaps they are coincidences, but they mean much to me.

In summary, the parables we have just studied imply that *the obsessively righteous and the obsessively sinful are not as different as is often thought.* Righteous and sinner alike are hopelessly "in debt" and in need of forgiveness. Both are invited to "relax," accept their imperfections and learn to live in more humble, forgiving, compassionate, "servant-like" ways. "Be merciful even as your Father is merciful" (Luke 6:36).

QUESTIONS FOR DISCUSSION AND FURTHER STUDY:

1. Am I a perfectionist? Do I see myself as better than others? Why? Why not?
2. How do I react to sins and weaknesses in my life? In the lives of others?
3. Is it possible to think both too highly of myself ("superiority complex") and too little ("inferiority complex")? How might such a condition bear upon the problem of excessive pride?

PART THREE

PARABLES EVOKING INSIGHT INTO RIGHT AND WRONG WAYS OF ACTING

Why do you call me "Lord, Lord," and not do what I tell you? (Luke 6:46)

VII. NO ACTION

20. THE TWO SONS (Matt. 21:28-32)

(a) Getting oriented

In the parables studied to this point two major themes were struck:

(1) The kingdom of God is near (Part One). A compassionate, gracious power is at work in human affairs. This power is present like the silent growth of seed, like the blossoming of a fig tree, like the inward permeation of leaven, like wheat breaking ground in spite of an overgrowth of weeds. This power is God whose love exceeds by far that of human friend or helper (the Wicked Judge!).

(2) God's compassion reaches out to good and bad alike (Part Two). Yes, God is the God of the righteous, but he is also God of the wayward and rejoices more over one "sinner" who repents than over ninety-nine "righteous" who need no repentance. The truth is, however, that even the righteous have "debts" they cannot pay and the most despised virtues that put the best of men to shame (the Good Samaritan). Many of these parables, as we have seen, were spoken defensively in response to Jesus' Pharisaic critics.

The stories to which we now turn, in this third and final section of our study, were no doubt addressed to this same group, but here a new theme emerges. Virtually all of the remaining parables portray individuals caught up in a spectrum of right and wrong actions and

103

reactions. In some instances the focal figures seem to want to avoid acting at all, while at the same time trying to cover up their do-nothing attitude with polite rationalizations. Others act, but in churlish, reckless, self-defeating ways. Only a few of these parables point to actions of a more meaningful kind.

In the background of these parables we can sense a growing hostility on the part of the Jewish religious elite toward Jesus' mission. The parables themselves intimate how deeply Jesus felt about the importance of that mission and how concerned he was that his contemporaries, in threatening to reject it, might be missing out on an event of decisive significance for their future as God's people.

We will begin this section of our study by looking at a group of parables where *failure to act at all* is the recurrent motif. In the parable of the Two Sons both this theme and its setting in the life of Jesus are made explicit.

(d) Getting acquainted with the text

In Matthew 21:28–32 parable and setting are tightly interwoven. According to Matthew 21:23 the parable's audience was made up of "priests and elders." After telling the parable Jesus asked for a response, and responds to the response with an interpretation. This interpretation is harmonious with everything we otherwise know about the mission of Jesus and merits our close attention.

> What do you think? A man had two sons; and he went to the first and said, "Son, go and work in the vineyard today." And he answered, "I will not"; but afterward he repented and went.
>
> And he went to the second and said the same; and he answered, "I go, sir," but did not go.
>
> Which of the two did the will of his father?
>
> They said, "The first."
>
> Jesus said to them, "Truly, I say to you, the tax collectors and the harlots go into the kingdom of God before you. For John came to you in the way of righteousness, and you did not believe him, but the tax collectors and the har-

lots believed him; and even when you saw it, you did not afterward repent and believe him."

The parable itself reminds us of the story of the Prodigal Son, where we also read of a father with two sons, one of them submissive, the other rebellious. The outwardly submissive son (in the above parable) is very polite ("I go, sir!") but does not do what the father tells him to do. The other son flaunts his father's command ("I will not!") but has second thoughts. In the end he goes to work, as the father said he should.

"Which of the two did the will of the father?" The question is not as easy to answer as it might at first seem. Both sons have misbehaved. The one was discourteous, the other disobedient. The parable's original audience is compelled to do some thinking ("What do you think?"), and Jesus does not continue until they have given their judgment in the matter.

(c) Deciding which text to study

Since only Matthew has recorded this parable, we must rely on his version alone, but there does not seem to be any serious problem in doing so (some textual traditions reverse the order of the sons). We should, of course, note the distinction between the parable proper and the attached comments which in this instance may well reflect the parable's original setting.

(d) Meaning in the setting of Jesus' life

Jesus' words interpreting this parable are full of emotion: "Truly, I say to you . . ." The burning issue was the attitude of the Jewish establishment toward the repentance movement initiated by John the Baptist. Unlike the tax collectors and harlots (who "go into the kingdom of God before you"), the religious elite were taking a very "stand offish" attitude. Rigorous in their devotion to Torah (law and tradition), ostensibly obedient ("I go, sir"), they were at the same time refusing to hear the word that God had spoken through John (cf. Luke 7:24–35). *This parable is an appeal to the leadership classes in Judaism to re-examine their passive "do-nothing" attitude toward the repentance movement spearheaded by John and now carried forward by Jesus.*

As previously, we will defer thinking about the relevance of this parable for our time until we have looked at all the parables that relate to this theme.

21. THE BARREN FIG TREE (Luke 13:6–9)

(a) Getting oriented

Like the parable just studied the parable of the Barren Fig Tree also speaks of "no action." A tree that normally bears much fruit is in this instance fruitless.

(b) Getting acquainted with the text

A man had a fig tree planted in his vineyard; and he came seeking fruit on it and found none.

And he said to the vinedresser, "Lo, these three years I have come seeking fruit on this fig tree, and I find none. Cut it down; why should it use up the ground?"

And he answered him, "Let it alone, sir, this year also, till I dig about it and put on manure. And if it bears fruit next year, well and good; but if not, you can cut it down."

It is not unusual for a fig tree to be planted in a vineyard. Such a tree would normally bear three crops a year and could be counted on for fruit when the grape harvest was meager. It is understandable, then, that the man in the parable is perturbed when he finds that the fig tree he had planted in his vineyard is completely fruitless. Fig trees mature in three years and he has come looking for fruit an additional three years. The tree must be six years old already. And still no fruit! "Cut it down; why should it use up the ground?" The root system of a fig tree is extensive and it uses a great deal of water.

The gardener is certainly going the extra mile when he suggests that the barren tree should be given another year to prove itself, while he digs about and fertilizes it. One rarely needed to treat a fig tree in such a special way.

(c) Deciding which text to study

The text of this parable presents no special problems. We can take it as Luke records it.

(d) Meaning in the setting of Jesus' life

We do not know on what occasion Jesus told this parable. Luke suggests vaguely that it was spoken "to the multitudes" (Luke 12:54). But it seems to have a sharper focus than that. The fruitless fig tree reminds us of the "fruitless" Jewish elite who were so callous to the new things happening (through John and Jesus) among the repentant tax collectors and sinners. Their lack of compassion for sinners could have dire consequences. True, the story ends on a note of "extended time." There will be one more chance and every effort will be made to win a favorable response. But if there is still no fruit, no response, no action on the part of the establishment, the ax will have to fall.

22. THE BANQUET
(Matt. 22:1–14/Luke 14:16–24/Thomas 64)

(a) Getting oriented

"No action " is again clearly the theme of the parable of the Banquet. A meal invitation is turned down right and left. Of course polite excuses are given. This parable takes us further than the previous ones into the attitudes behind the peculiar complacency that infected upper-class Jewish life.

(b) Getting acquainted with the texts

The textual variations in the three available versions of this parable are most interesting. They illustrate graphically the way a parable could change its form and meaning in the process of transmission (see our discussion of this point in the Introduction, "Why differing versions of the same parable?").

Matt. 22:1–14	Luke 14:16–24	Thomas 64
The kingdom of heaven may be compared to a king who gave a marriage feast for his son, and sent his servants to call those who were invited to the marriage feast; but they would not come. Again he sent other servants, saying, "Tell those who are invited, Behold, I have made ready my dinner, my oxen and my fat calves are killed, and everything is ready; come to the marriage feast." But they made light of it and went off, one to his farm, another to his business, while the rest seized his servants, treated them shamefully, and killed them. The king was angry, and he sent his troops and destroyed those murderers and burned their city. Then he said to his servants, "The wedding is ready, but those invited were not worthy. Go therefore to the thoroughfares, and invite to the marriage feast as many as you find." And those servants went out into the streets and gathered all whom they found, both bad and good; so the wedding hall was filled with	A man once gave a great banquet, and invited many; and at the time of the banquet he sent his servant to say to those who had been invited, "Come; for all is now ready." But they all alike began to make excuses. The first said to him, "I have bought a field, and I must go out and see it; I pray you, have me excused." And another said, "I have bought five yoke of oxen, and I go to examine them; I pray you, have me excused." And another said, "I have married a wife, and therefore I cannot come." So the servant came and reported this to his master. Then the householder in anger said to his servant, "Go out quickly to the streets and lanes of the city, and bring in the poor and maimed and blind and lame." And the servant said, "Sir, what you have commanded has been done, and still there is room." And the master said to the servant "Go out to the highways and hedges, and compel people to come in, that my house may be filled. For I	A man had guests, and when he had prepared the dinner, he sent his servant to summon the guests. He came to the first; he said to him: My master summons thee. He said: I have money with some merchants. They are coming to me in the evening. I will go and give them orders. I pray to be excused from the dinner. He went to another; he said to him: My master has summoned thee. He said to him: I have bought a house and they ask me for a day. I shall not have time. He came to another; he said to him: My master summons thee. He said to him: My friend is about to be married, and I am to hold a dinner. I shall not be able to come. I pray to be excused from the dinner. He went to another; he said to him: My master summons thee; He said to him: I have bought a village; I go to collect the rent. I shall not be able to come. I pray to be excused. The servant came, he said to his master: Those whom thou didst summon to the dinner have excused themselves.

guests. But when the king came in to look at the guests, he saw there a man who had no wedding garment; and he said to him, "Friend, how did you get in here without a wedding garment?" And he was speechless. Then the king said to the attendants, "Bind him hand and foot, and cast him into the outer darkness; there men will weep and gnash their teeth." For many are called, but few are chosen.

tell you, none of those men who were invited shall taste my banquet."

The master said to his servant: Go out to the road. Bring those whom thou shalt find, that they may dine. The buyers and the merchants [shall] not [enter] the places of my father.

In sorting out the variations, it might be well to look at the biggest difference first of all: the extra scene at the end of Matthew's version of this parable. All three versions tell of a host who prepared a meal, invited guests who refused to come, and who then invited other guests. But only Matthew tells us that when all the guests had arrived, the host went and inspected them, and upon seeing a man there inappropriately dressed (perhaps too sloppy or dirty) had him thrown out. This looks like a somewhat artificial addition. In any case it makes no sense, at a literal level, for the King to take offense at a guest's attire when he had more or less compelled him to come to the wedding banquet at the last minute and right off the street!

This striking difference in the ending of the parable in Matthew alerts us to other peculiarities in the way he tells the story. His host is a "King" (just a "man" in Luke and Thomas), and the meal a "marriage feast for his son" (a "great banquet" in Luke, simply a "dinner" in Thomas). The King in Matthew sends out "servants" (only one "servant" in Luke and Thomas). He sends them twice to the originally invited guests (only once in Luke and Thomas). On the second sending the servants are mocked, persecuted and killed (politely refused in Luke and Thomas). Then (while the meal is still waiting!) the King mobilizes his troops and destroys these guests who refused his invitation, and burns down "their city." This action is completely missing in Luke and Thomas. All three, however, report a second invitation to a new group of guests. Only Luke's version adds that even this second effort was only partially successful in filling the banquet hall. According to Luke the servant had to go on a third mission outside of the city to "the highways and hedges."

How are we to explain these many differences, especially those between Matthew and the other versions? It would appear that Matthew has done two things with the original story: (1) He has reshaped it into an allegory; and (2) he has combined it with a second parable.

His allegorical handling of the story is fairly transparent. The king is God. The son is Jesus. The marriage banquet is the age to come. The "servants" who *first* summoned the invited guests are possibly meant to symbolize the prophets sent by God to Israel. The "other servants" are the apostles and early Christians. These were mocked and persecuted (by the Jews) but their "king" (God) punished the Jewish people for doing this by sending (Roman) armies to wipe them out and destroy "their city" (Jerusalem).

After this the invitations are directed to those outside of Jerusalem. The original parable ended here on a somewhat problematical note (so far as Matthew was concerned): "both bad and good" are gathered into the banquet hall! Viewed allegorically from the standpoint of the early church, this might look as though "good and bad" alike have a place in the "kingdom of heaven" (Matt. 22:2). To correct this impression Matthew added another parable: The parable of the Guest without a Wedding Garment. It too is read by Matthew as an allegory. The King coming "to look at his guests" prefigures the coming day of judgment when those who have entered the church under false pretenses and without a proper "garment" (way of life) will be taken by God, bound and thrown into "outer darkness."

In Matthew the original parable has become an allegory depicting the whole course of salvation history from the time of the pre-Christian prophets, to the first Christian mission to Jerusalem (and its rejection by the Jews), to the destruction of Jerusalem, the mission of the church beyond Jerusalem and on to the coming day of judgment.

The story as Luke and Thomas tell it is a far simpler one, although Luke too seems to have added an allegorical touch when he describes *two* missions (following the rejection by the original guests) instead of one (as in Matthew and Thomas). Is this because he wants this parable to point beyond the mission to the Jews outside of Jerusalem (Judea and Samaria) to the Gentile mission as well (in accordance with the threefold commission in Acts 1:8)?

In any case the original story in its barest outline must have been fairly straightforward. A moderately wealthy man invites guests to a meal. When the meal is prepared, those who had previously accepted his invitation are informed that all is now ready. This latter courtesy was apparently customary at that time in Jerusalem among upper-class hosts (Jeremias). Matthew, Luke and Thomas differ about who the invited guests were and the specific nature of their responses. But they agree that they were all well-to-do, very busy, and for the most part very polite. At the same time every last one of them excused himself in a patently rationalizing manner.

Small wonder that the host is angry and on an impulse sends his servant into the streets to invite others.

(c) Deciding which text to study

From what has been said, it is apparent that the choice of texts in this instance is important. If we wish to know how this parable was reshaped and understood by certain early Christians, we should study Matthew's version. But then we will not learn much about what the parable might have meant originally when first spoken by Jesus. For that we must turn to Luke or Thomas.

(d) Meaning in the setting of Jesus' life

According to Luke this is another one of those parables that Jesus told rather spontaneously during the course of a meal in the home of an upper-class Pharisee (Luke 14:1). A guest "who sat at table with him" (Luke 14:15) had just exclaimed: "Blessed is he who shall eat bread in the kingdom of God." Jesus must have sensed something false in this pious sentiment. Was it too smug? Was it too cocksure? Did the man who uttered it too easily assume that *he* would be among those who "shall eat bread in the kingdom of God"?

In any case our parable sounds a warning. "You may *think* you have said yes to God. But what if you are like those men who were invited to a banquet, accepted it, but then when the meal was actually ready, were too snobbish and too busy to attend? What if others whom you now despise take your place? (A popular folktale of that day told of just such an event. A wealthy tax collector shortly before his death gave just such a feast to ingratiate himself with his upper-class acquaintances, only to find that they all snubbed him. In anger he sent his servant out into the streets to invite beggars. For additional details, see pages 118f.)

"Therefore take care, you polite, self-righteous Pharisees. Take care that in your aloof busyness with fields and oxen and wives [Luke], with money, houses, wedding feasts, and capital investments [Thomas], with farms and commerce [Matthew], you do not miss out on what God is now doing. If you do, tax collectors and harlots might indeed find their way into the kingdom of God before you."

23. MONEY ON CREDIT
(Matt. 25:14–30/Luke 19:12–27)

(a) Getting oriented

In the parable of the Talents (as it is traditionally called) there are three slaves to whom sums of money were entrusted. Two of them put their money to work. The third is a striking example of the theme: "no action." He buried his money in the ground. All emphasis in the parable falls on this third slave and his fate.

(b) Getting acquainted with the texts

The two available versions of this parable display an unusual number of variations. It is beyond the scope of our present study to try to identify or explain all of them. Those who have done so agree that Matthew's version is the more authentic. Luke has complicated the original parable by adding a historical reminiscence (familiar to his contemporaries) about a "nobleman" (Herod's son Archelaus) who went into a far country (Rome) "to receive kingly power" (get his kingship over Judea confirmed). The citizens hated this nobleman and tried to have him dethroned. They were unsuccessful in this, and upon his return ("having received kingly power") he took out his vengeance against those who did not want him to reign over them (Luke 19:27). None of this is in Matthew's version.

Matthew 25:14–30	Luke 19:12–27
For it will be as when a man going on a journey called his servants and entrusted to them his property; to one he gave five talents, to another two, to another one, to each according to his ability. Then he went away. He who had received the five talents went at once and traded with them; and he made five talents more. So also, he who had the two talents made two talents more. But he who had received the one talent went and dug in the ground and hid his master's money. Now after a long time the master of those servants came and settled accounts with them. And he who had received the five talents came forward, bringing five talents more, saying, "Master, you delivered to me five talents; here I have made five talents more." His master said to him, "Well done, good and faithful servant; you have been faithful over a little, I will set you over much; enter into the joy of your master." And he also who had the two talents came forward, saying, "Master, you delivered to me two talents; here I have made two talents more." His master said to him, "Well done, good and faithful servant; you have been faithful over a little, I will set you over much; enter into the joy of your master." He also who had received the one talent came forward, saying, "Master, I knew you to be a hard man, reaping where you did not sow and gathering where you did not winnow; so I was afraid, and I went and hid your talent in the ground. Here you have what is	A nobleman went into a far country to receive kingly power and then return. Calling ten of his servants, he gave them ten pounds, and said to them, "Trade with these till I come." But his citizens hated him and sent an embassy after him, saying, "We do not want this man to reign over us." When he returned, having received the kingly power, he commanded these servants, to whom he had given the money, to be called to him, that he might know what they had gained by trading. The first came before him, saying, "Lord, your pound has made ten pounds more." And he said to him, "Well done, good servant! Because you have been faithful in very little, you shall have authority over ten cities." And the second came, saying, "Lord, your pound has made five pounds." And he said to him, "And you are to be over five cities." Then another came, saying, "Lord, here is your pound, which I kept laid away in a napkin; for I was afraid of you, because you are a severe man; you take up what you did not lay down, and reap what you did not sow." He said to him, "I will condemn you out of your own mouth, you wicked servant! You knew that I was a severe man, taking up what I did not lay down and reaping what I did not sow? Why then did you not put my money into the bank, and at my coming I should have collected it with interest?" And he said to those who stood by, "Take the pound from

yours." But his master answered him, "You wicked and slothful servant! You knew that I reap where I have not sowed, and gather where I have not winnowed? Then you ought to have invested my money with bankers, and at my coming I should have received what was my own with interest. So take the talent from him, and give it to him who has ten talents.

For to every one who has will more be given, and he will have abundance; but from him who has not, even what he has will be taken away. And cast the worthless servant into the outer darkness; there men will weep and gnash their teeth."

him, and give it to him who has the ten pounds."
(And they said to him, "Lord, he has ten pounds!")
"I tell you, that to every one who has will more be given; but from him who has not, even what he has will be taken away.

But as for these enemies of mine, who did not want me to reign over them, bring them here and slay them before me."

Even though Matthew's text in general is the more original (as suggested above), Luke's version may help us correct it at a few points. For example, Luke's reckoning of the amount of money entrusted to the slaves (one pound or several hundred dollars each) might be more original than the amounts cited in Matthew (one, two, and five talents, with a talent equaling *thousands* of dollars). Would a master who had given a slave thousands of dollars commend him with the words: "You have been faithful over *a little* . . ."? Also the phrase, "enter into the joy ["banquet"] of your master" (in Matthew, but not Luke), sounds like a secondary flourish. Matthew would like us to read this parable as an allegory of judgment day. It is doubtful that this was its original intent (see below).

Both versions have the attached saying: "For to every one who has will more be given . . . but from him who has not, even what he has will be taken away." This maxim appears elsewhere in the Gospels as an independent saying (Matt. 13:12/Mark 4:25/Luke 8:18) and was probably not original to this parable. This is really not the parable's main point. Also the statements that follow this maxim in both versions look like secondary expansions. Matthew's "cast the worthless servant into the outer darkness . . ." appears only in his Gospel (Matt. 8:12 and 22:13) and nowhere else in the New Testament.

In all likelihood, then, the original parable ended with the master's stern command: "So take the talent [or pound] from him [the servant who hid it] and give it to him who has the ten talents [pounds]." The point is this: the servant who buried his money in the ground out of "fear" for his master was refusing to act in accord with the master's wishes. This servant should have known that his master would never approve such a miserly do-nothing attitude.

(d) Deciding which text to study

Matthew's version is the simpler and more natural telling of this story. The attached maxim however ("For to everyone who has . . .") and the verses that follow are probably secondary. It would appear that Luke has the more original version of the sums of money involved.

(e) Meaning in the setting of Jesus' life

Matthew places this parable among teachings Jesus supposedly gave his disiple about the "close of the age" (Matt. 24:3). This is in harmony with his opinion that the parable is an allegory of the last judgment.

Luke places it at the end of Jesus' final journey to Jerusalem when expectations were running high "that the kingdom of God was to appear immediately" (Luke 19:11). This may explain why he combined it with a story about a nobleman (Jesus) who went into a far country (the ascension of Jesus). For him it is an allegory of church history ("Trade with these till I come"), and counsels patience and endurance. The kingdom is not coming as soon as some might think.

Originally this parable may have had nothing to do with either of these situations. In its simplest form it sounds again like a story Jesus might have told as a warning to Jewish leaders who were increasingly hostile to the movement initiated by John the Baptist and Jesus. John and Jesus had released through their preaching a wave of repentance. Alienated Jews were finding their way back to God. But the Pharisaic establishment stood aloof from all this. They were threatened and fearful. Their attitude toward religion is accurately depicted in the outlook of the third servant. They looked upon God as a hard taskmaster ("I knew you to be a hard man . . .") and upon themselves as the anxious guardians of the Jewish religious heritage (Torah).

"Woe to you, scribes and Pharisees . . ." Jesus is reported to have said on another occasion, "because you shut the kingdom of heaven against men; for you neither enter yourselves, nor allow those who would enter to go in" (Matt. 23:13/Luke 11:52).

24. THE RICH FOOL
(Luke 12:16–21/Thomas 63)

(a) Getting oriented

In the parable of the Banquet men excuse themselves from attending a meal because of their rather snobbish attitudes and typically middle-class preoccupations. In the parable of the Money on Credit the leading figure is so bent on security that he hides the money given him in the ground. Wealth and the drive for security are also features of the story of the "Rich Fool."

(b) Getting acquainted with the texts

In Luke this parable has a concluding maxim: "So is he who lays up treasure for himself, and is not rich toward God" (Luke 12:21). As we have seen, generalizing conclusions of this type, on closer inspection, almost always prove to be later additions. In this instance too that would seem to be the case, for not only is this maxim absent from Thomas, but it interprets the parable as though it were a moral example: "Do not be selfish with your wealth as this rich man was." Is this really what this parable is all about?

Luke 12:16b–21	Thomas 63
The land of a rich man brought forth plentifully; and he thought to himself, "What shall I do, for I have nowhere to store my crops?"	There was a rich man who had much property.

And he said, "I will do this: I will pull down my barns, and build larger ones; and there I will store all my grain and my goods. And I will say to my soul, Soul, you have ample goods laid up for many years; take your ease, eat, drink, be merry."

He said: "I will use my property that I may sow and reap and plant and fill my storehouses with fruit, so that I lack nothing." That was what he thought in his heart.

But God said to him, "Fool! This night your soul is required of you; and the things you have prepared, whose will they be?" So is he who lays up treasure for himself, and is not rich toward God.

And that night he died. Whoever has ears let him hear.

There are subtle but significant differences between the way Luke and Thomas tell this story. Both describe a rich man, but in Luke he is trying to decide what to do with an excess of farm produce, while in Thomas he ponders how to invest his "much property." The one determines to tear down his barns and build bigger ones (Luke), the other to increase his farming operation in order to fill his storehouses (Thomas). The one is driven by a desire for luxurious living ("Take your ease . . ."), the other by the quest for total security (". . . so that I lack nothing"). Luke's parable ends with "God" making an ironical prediction ("Fool! This night . . ."). Thomas simply tells us that on the night this man decided to make himself secure he died.

Was this parable originally about a man who decided to tear down his barns and build bigger ones in order to live in luxury, or about a man whose driving ambition was to fill his barns and find security? Both versions are possible, but the entry of "God" into Luke's version arouses suspicions, as does his moralizing conclusion. No other parable of Jesus has God entering the story in this explicit manner.

(c) Deciding which text to study

The Thomas version, with its emphasis on the rich man's quest for an anxiety-free existence, fits in better with what is otherwise known about the issues that engaged Jesus in his public mission than does Luke's. Also the abrupt ending in Thomas ("And that night he died") is preferable to Luke's atypical God speech. Both versions present valuable teaching. The story as Thomas has it is probably closer to the original.

(d) Meaning in the setting of Jesus' life

Both the Gospel setting to which Luke has assigned this parable as well as his moralizing preface (Luke 12:15) and conclusion (Luke 12:21) make it clear that for him this parable was straightforward teaching against avarice.

The Thomas version suggests another possibility. In his characterization of the rich man we are once again reminded of the Pharisees. They are like men of great wealth whose main goal in life is to "lack nothing." This perfectionist ambition alarmed Jesus, because it was so self-serving and so oblivious to the crying needs of the time (the pathetic alienation of the disaffiliated). Furthermore, do the religious elite realize that with all their wealth and ambition they stand on the brink of a catastrophe?

25. THE RICH MAN AND LAZARUS
(Luke 16:19–31)

(a) Getting oriented

Here is another rich man who failed to wake up to the real issues of life before it was too late. He died blind to what he had done and what he had failed to do. But in this instance the story does not end there. It goes on to examine the deeper reasons for this failure to act.

(b) Getting acquainted with the text

Some background information is important if we are not to go off on false tangents. First of all, it is worth knowing that this particular parable draws upon contemporary folklore. Joachim Jeremias informs us that in the Aramaic Talmud there is a story about a rich tax collector named Ma'jan who died and was given a splendid funeral. At the same time a poor scholar died and no one attended his funeral. The question is asked why God allowed this. Upon investigation it is discovered that the rich man had done a good deed just before his death. When no one of his upper-class friends showed up at a banquet he had prepared, he decided to fill his banquet hall with the poor (this part of the story, as we have already seen, is used by Jesus in his parable of the Banquet.) But the story does not end here. In the afterlife (as seen in a dream by one of his colleagues) the scholar who had fared so poorly on earth is described as living in a land of paradise-like beauty, while Bar Ma'jan, the publican, stands on the bank of a stream trying unsuccessfully to reach the water.

In other words, many of the "trappings" of this story are traditional. They are not original with Jesus and do not necessarily tell us anything about his view of the afterlife.

Furthermore, this is one of four two-part parables (the other three are the Prodigal Son, the Banquet and the Generous Employer). In all of these parables the emphasis seems to fall on the second part. As we study this parable, then, we should view the setting as folkloric and expect to find the parable's thrust in its final section.

There was a rich man, who was clothed in purple and fine linen and who feasted sumptuously every day. And at his gate lay a poor man named Lazarus, full of sores, who desired to be fed with what fell from the rich man's table; moreover the dogs came and licked his sores.

The poor man died and was carried by the angels to Abraham's bosom.

The rich man also died and was buried; and in Hades, being in torment, he lifted up his eyes, and saw Abraham far off and Lazarus in his bosom. And he called out, "Father Abraham, have mercy upon me, and send Lazarus to dip the end of his finger in water and cool my tongue; for I am in anguish in this flame."

But Abraham said, "Son, remember that you in your lifetime received your good things, and Lazarus in like manner evil things; but now he is comforted here, and you are in anguish. And besides all this, between us and you a great chasm has been fixed, in order that those who would pass from here to you may not be able, and none may cross there to us."

And he said, "Then I beg you, father, to send him to my father's house, for I have five brothers, so that he may warn them, lest they also come into this place of torment."

But Abraham said, "They have Moses and the prophets; let them hear them."

And he said, "No, father Abraham; but if some one goes to them from the dead, they will repent."

He said to him, "If they do not hear Moses and the prophets, neither will they be convinced if some one should rise from the dead."

The opening paragraph impresses upon us the contrasting lifestyles of the rich man and Lazarus. The treatment that Lazarus receives at the rich man's hands is not, however, as shocking as it might at first appear. The rich man has kindly permitted him to beg at his gate, and "what fell from the rich man's table" was no doubt more than crumbs. But still the economic, social and physical disparities are atrocious.

All this, however, is only background for another scene: the reversal of fortunes in the afterlife, and especially the dialogue that takes place there between the rich man and Abraham. This dialogue is really quite astonishing. It has a tongue-in-cheek quality that one does not usually associate with Jesus. Notice how courteously they address one another across that great gulf that separates them ("Father Abraham . . . !" "Son . . . !") Notice too how rationally (in the light of their circumstances) they converse about the issues between them. Moving from topic to topic they suddenly come upon the problem of the rich man's five brothers. "If only Lazarus might be sent back to warn them of their fate!" But Abraham will not hear of it: "They have Moses and the prophets." "No, father Abraham . . ." the rich man shouts. He will not let this idea die so quickly. A dramatic event like the return of Lazarus from the dead would surely bring his brothers to repentance. But Abraham is adamant and brings the conversation to an abrupt close by repeating with categorical finality: "If they do not hear Moses and the prophets, neither will they be convinced if some one should rise from the dead."

(c) Deciding which text to study

Only Luke records this rather unusual parable, so we must rely completely on the veracity of his account of it. There doesn't seem to be any serious reason not to do so.

(d) Meaning in the setting of Jesus' life

The parable of the Rich Man and Lazarus unwinds slowly, but there can be no doubt toward what it is unwinding: how to break through the shell of indifference that surrounds five rich brothers of the rich man in Hades?

In these five brothers, we can see once again a picture of the wealthy, upper-class religious elite who were so callous to Jesus' message of the kingdom and so offended by his association with riffraff.

Is there any way to break through their cool disdain toward the poor? Only by way of ordinary communication, this parable seems to suggest, not by any special tricks. "They have Moses and the prophets; let them hear them." If in daily contact with their sacred scriptures the wealthy do not know that their treatment of the poor is wrong, it is because they do not listen. And if they do not listen to their own holy scriptures, they will not listen to anyone else. ". . . the breakdown in communication is due to the unwillingness of the rich to hear" (Granskou). The analysis is perceptive and made just a little more palatable perhaps by being whimsically ascribed to "Father Abraham," who shouts it to one of his "Sons" in Hades.

(e) Listening to the parables today

Complacency—that is what we can sense behind every one of the parables we have just studied: Indecisiveness due to complacency. And complacency of a very special vintage—the complacency of those who are proper, wealthy and religious.

Each of these parables raises a question that goes straight to the heart of our modern situation. For we too face a crisis due to complacency—and this among those who are proper, wealthy and religious.

Almost everywhere we look today we can see the lines hardening between the strong and the weak, between wealthy and poor, between the righteous and sinners. And those who consolidate their strength against the weak only too often turn out to be the religious, who also profess to be defenders of decency (law and order).

I see myself in this group. I am well salaried. I have leisure to write this book. I have been a law-abiding citizen. I worship God according to the Christian tradition. I do not want to give up any of these things. I like my life-style and become vaguely anxious as I sense the crisis toward which this globe seems to be drifting. News of poverty in the third world, news of violence, emotional illness, and crime in our urban ghettos—I would rather not hear of it. A voice whispers, "There's nothing much you can do about it anyway. You're living a good life. Don't worry yourself." Complacency!

Will tax collectors and harlots, politicians and social workers enter the kingdom of God before I do? Is compassion and love breaking out more decisively and helpfully among "sinners" than among me and my kind?

To what extent am I saying "yes" to God and then turning around and living just as I please (the parable of the Two Sons)?

To what extent am I saying "yes" to God and then snobbishly excusing myself from actual involvement in the significant movements of my time, because of my preoccupation with "business as usual" (the parable of the Banquet)?

To what extent have I simply taken the rich heritage of faith that is mine and "preserved" it, rather than putting it to work for others (the parable of Money on Credit)?

To what extent am I so preoccupied with security and pleasure that I am simply not able to discern the "signs of the times" (the parable of the Rich Fool)?

To what extent have I closed my ears to all moral and spiritual correction (the law and the prophets), so that I am impervious to change (the parable of the Rich Man and Lazarus)?

VIII. SELF-DEFEATING ACTION

26. CHILDREN IN THE MARKET PLACE
(Matt. 11:16–19/Luke 7:31–35)

(a) Getting oriented

When I wrote in the previous chapter of the religious establishment failing to act in response to the message of John the Baptist and Jesus, this was only partly correct. An authentic challenge *demands* action. Even "no action" is a form of acting. To say "I cannot come" is also a decision.

And if the challenge persists and the lack of response continues, "no action" will eventually stand fully disclosed for what it is: rejection (self-defeating rejection where important issues are at stake).

The parables to which we now turn depict people acting in self-defeating, irresponsible and rejecting ways.

(b) Getting acquainted with the texts

The differences between the two available versions of this parable are small and with one exception not very significant.

Matthew 11:16–19	Luke 7:31–35
But to what shall I compare this generation? It is like children sitting in the market places and calling to their playmates, "We piped to you, and you did not dance; we wailed, and you did not mourn." For John came neither eating	To what then shall I compare the men of this generation, and what are they like? They are like children sitting in the market place and calling to one another, "We piped to you, and you did not dance; we wailed, and you did not

nor drinking, and they say, "He has a demon"; the Son of man came eating and drinking, and they say, "Behold, a glutton and a drunkard, a friend of tax collectors and sinners!" Yet wisdom is justified by her deeds.

weep." For John the Baptist has come eating no bread and drinking no wine; and you say, "He has a demon." The Son of man has come eating and drinking; and you say, "Behold, a glutton and a drunkard, a friend of tax collectors and sinners!

Yet wisdom is justified by all her children."

This is another instance where parable and interpretation have been transmitted together. The picture of children squabbling at their games is a symbol of "this generation," we are told, and more specifically of those who stand aloof from both John the Baptist and Jesus and critically attack them.

But where in the parable itself is the metaphorical thrust? A small variation in the texts should be noted before answering. In Luke it is said that the children are *sitting* and "calling to one another." In Matthew these children are also said to be sitting but they are calling "to their playmates." Matthew in this instance provides a slightly sharper focus on what is happening. The children on the ground are not calling to each other but to their playmates who are standing and playing. In other words, there are two groups of children represented here, those *sitting* passively on the ground, piping and wailing, and those *standing* who are supposed to respond.

But the group that is sitting is full of complaints. Their more active playmates ignore their suggestions. They won't play either "wedding" or "funeral."

It is not altogether clear what is meant by the final sentence in Jesus' interpretation: Yet wisdom is justified "by her deeds" (Matthew), "by all her children" (Luke). It may mean that the wise conduct of those who have repented in response to the message of Jesus and John is proof against the carping criticism of the religious establishment.

(c) Deciding which text to study

For reasons indicated, Matthew's text gives a slightly clearer version of this parable, but the two texts are remarkably similar.

(d) Meaning in the setting of Jesus' life

Jesus is perturbed by the superficiality (childishness) of the Jewish establishment's response to both John's movement and his own. In their eyes John's life-style was too severe, Jesus' too lax. The one they explained away as being mentally deranged ("He has a demon"), the other as being morally loose ("Behold, a glutton and a drunkard, a friend of tax collectors and sinners"). These are the kinds of shallow, self-righteous judgments that men in power are prone to make against those who do not wholly conform to their way of thinking. Jesus wants to challenge this attitude. At the same time he is confident that the "deeds" of those being criticized will prevail against it.

Again we will wait to discuss the contemporary relevance of this parable until we have studied the other parables in this group.

27. RETURN OF THE UNCLEAN SPIRIT
(Matt. 12:43–45b/Luke 11:24–26)

(a) Getting oriented

Questions have been raised as to whether the "Return of the Unclean Spirit" is a parable at all. It could be read literally as a comment on demon exorcism. Then its meaning would be that the casting out of an unclean spirit is not enough in and of itself. Something must replace the departed demon, or it will return with others.

But Matthew's version of this story ends: "So shall it be with this evil generation." Luke too has placed it in a context of conflict with "this evil generation" (Luke 11:29). For them, the story of the Return of the Unclean Spirit carried a subtle warning for contemporary Judaism.

(b) Getting acquainted with the texts

The two versions of this parable are remarkably similar.

Matthew 12:43–45	Luke 11:24–26
When the unclean spirit has gone out of a man, he passes through waterless places seeking rest, but he finds none.	When the unclean spirit has gone out of a man, he passes through waterless places seeking rest; and finding none he

Then he says, "I will return to my house from which I came." And when he comes he finds it empty, swept, and put in order. Then he goes and brings with him seven other spirits more evil than himself, and they enter and dwell there; and the last state of that man becomes worse than the first. So shall it be also with this evil generation.

says, "I will return to my house from which I came." And when he comes he finds it swept and put in order. Then he goes and brings seven other spirits more evil than himself, and they enter and dwell there; and the last state of that man becomes worse than the first.

"Unclean spirit" is the Palestinian way of referring to a demon, and these "unclean spirits" were thought to live in desert ("waterless") places. "The comparison of a possessed person to the 'house' of a demon is still common in the East" (Jeremias). The house that the demon vacated was "empty, swept and put in order" (Matthew). This inviting prospect is what prompted the critical turn of events that is the point of this particular story. Exuberant at finding such a hospitable place to lodge, the demon goes and finds seven spirits "more evil than himself," and together they return to dwell in this poor man. "So shall it be also with this evil generation."

(c) Deciding which text to study

Either text can be used in the study of this parable, since they are so similar (although Matthew's addition of the word "empty" to the description of the house may be an authentic touch).

(d) Meaning in the setting of Jesus' life

If Matthew is correct in suggesting that this peculiar story about an enterprising demon is a parable having to do with "this evil generation," then the words "empty, swept, and put in order" take on a peculiar pathos. They express something of how Jesus must have felt about Pharisaic Judaism (the dominant party among the Jews of that time). The demons had departed. Zeal for righteousness had certainly swept the house of Judaism clean and put everything in order. But Jesus noticed that in spite of all this the Jewish religious establishment was vacuous. It could criticize other movements (see the previous parable), but it was powerless to do much itself by way of helping the masses. It lacked life, vitality, compassion. And lacking these it was susceptible to reinfiltration by destructive forces far worse than those it rejected.

28. THE TEN VIRGINS (Matt. 25:1–13)

(a) Getting oriented

The parable of the Ten Virgins has such a long history of being read as an allegory of the "close of the age" (Matt. 24:3) that it is difficult to see it in any other light. Doesn't, after all, the parable's final admonition tell us to "Watch, for you know neither the day nor the hour," and isn't this a clear reference to the second coming of Christ? Well then, the bridegroom in the parable must be a symbol of the Messiah, and the virgins represent the church.

But Biblical scholars suggest that it would have been impossible for Jesus' original audiences to have understood the parable in this way. To speak of the Messiah as a bridegroom was totally foreign to the Jews of Jesus' day. This symbol first came into use among the early Christians (II Cor. 11:2). It is evident too that the main point of the original parable was not about "watching," for both the wise and the foolish virgins fall asleep while waiting for the bridegroom. What divided the ten maidens into two groups was not that one group "watched" and the other didn't, but that five of them were prepared and five not. The story focuses on those who were poorly prepared. This is another parable about persons involved in self-defeating action.

(b) Getting acquainted with the text

It is unfortunate that we do not have more than Matthew's version of this parable. From our previous study of the parables of the Weeds among the Wheat and the Banquet we know how prone Matthew was to embellish the tradition allegorically, especially (as here) where a parable seemed to relate to the coming day of judgment. To what extent has the text of this parable been changed? Lacking a parallel version, we cannot say for sure.

Our approach then will have to be to take the parable very much as Matthew has recorded it, but without the concluding admonition to "watch" (which misses the parable's point—see above), and with special caution against reading it as an allegory.

The kingdom of heaven shall be compared to ten maidens who took their lamps and went to meet the bridegroom. Five of them were foolish, and five were wise. For when the foolish took their lamps, they took no oil with them; but the wise took flasks of oil with their lamps. As the bridegroom was delayed, they all slumbered and slept. But at midnight there was a cry "Behold, the bridegroom! Come out to meet him." Then all those maidens rose and trimmed their lamps. And the foolish said to the wise, "Give us some of your oil, for our lamps are going out." But the wise replied, "Perhaps there will not be enough for us and for you; go rather to the dealers and buy for yourselves." And while they went to buy, the bridegroom came, and those who were ready went in with him to the marriage feast; and the door was shut. Afterward the other maidens came also, saying, "Lord, lord, open to us." But he replied, "Truly, I say to you, I do not know you."

Joachim Jeremias has gone to great pains to establish the credibility of this story. This kind of thing actually could and did happen at Palestinian weddings. The bride-to-be waited at home with her wedding party (the ten maidens), while the bridegroom negotiated elsewhere with her relatives the various financial details involved in obtaining her as his wife. It was a mark of respect on all sides to prolong this bargaining. It showed how much both parents and bridegroom valued the girl in question. This is all that is involved in the otherwise cryptic words: "As the bridegroom was delayed . . ." (which may have prompted the early Christian interpretation of this parable as an allegory of the "delayed" second coming of Christ).

As the story unfolds the focus centers more and more on the folly of those maidens who did not have the foresight to bring an extra flask of oil. They should have anticipated that the bridegroom would be delayed (he always was!), and that their lamps (which were burning while they slept) might run dry. When the inevitable happened, there was a great commotion. The foolish maidens first try to borrow from the others, but those who brought an extra flask of oil will not hear of it. They might run out too! So off the silly girls go looking for an oil dealer (in the middle of the night!), but by the time they return, it is too late. The bridegroom has already entered the house, the door is shut and festivities are already in full swing. When they try to get in, the bridegroom refuses. Barring a door was no simple task, and guests who did not arrive on time could not expect to be admitted to such a gala affair.

(c) Deciding which text to study

It only needs to be emphasized again that if we want to know what Jesus meant in telling this story, it should be read, not as an allegory, but as a simple story with a single metaphorical thrust.

(d) Meaning in the setting of Jesus' life

This story reminds us of the Banquet parable. There too people miss out on festivities, but simply because they would not come. Here the people come (they act), but in a foolish self-defeating way. The foolish maidens are careless. They really do not take the wedding all that seriously and make the necessary preparations.

Is Jesus again saying something about the responses being accorded his movement? A new spirit was being spread abroad in the hearts and minds of many "lost" Jews. "Sinners" were finding their way back to God. Healing was taking place. A new era for Judaism seemed to be dawning. The kingdom of God was "coming upon you," but too many of Jesus' contemporaries (the leaders especially) were responding like silly girls at a wedding waiting to greet the bridegroom without an extra flask of oil for their lamps. The Jewish establishment just wasn't taking seriously what was happening among them.

29. THE GUEST WITHOUT A WEDDING GARMENT (Matt. 22:2, 11–14)

(a) Getting oriented

The reasons for viewing this story as a self-contained parable (rather than as part of the parable of the Banquet) were cited previously in our study of the Banquet parable (see pp. 109f. for details). The parallel versions of the Banquet parable (in Luke and Thomas) do not have it, and it does not really fit that story.

Looked at in its own right, the parable of the Guest without a Wedding Garment continues the theme: self-defeating action. Once again we are told of a man who behaved without appropriate forethought.

(b) Getting acquainted with the text

Joachim Jeremias suggests that the opening verse of this parable might be Matthew 22:2, the beginning sentence of the Banquet parable. If this is correct, it explains how the parable of the "great banquet" (Luke) became the parable of the king's "marriage feast" (Matthew).

The parable originally must have ended with the king ordering his "attendants" to remove the offending individual from the wedding hall. The phrases, "into outer darkness," and "there men will weep and gnash their teeth" (13b) reappear in Matthew's versions of several other parables (Matt. 24:51c; 25:30). In those instances they are missing in the parallel texts (Luke 12:46c; Luke 19:27). We may assume that they are secondary here as well.

With these suggestions in mind the text of this parable would read as follows:

> The kingdom of heaven may be compared to a king who gave a marriage feast for his son . . . [v. 2]
> But when the king came in to look at the guests, he saw there a man who had no wedding garment; and he said to him, "Friend, how did you get in here without a wedding garment?"

And he was speechless.
Then the king said to the attendants, "Bind him hand
and foot, and cast him out . . ." [vv. 11–13a]

One can hardly imagine a more splendid event than a king's banquet for his son's wedding. It is an especially fine moment when the guests have arrived, all decked out in their finery and the king moves among them, greeting and welcoming them.

But suddenly the king is confronted by a man sloppily dressed. So far as we know there was no special garment for weddings. What angers the king is that this wretched man's clothing is inappropriate to a festive occasion of this nature.

The king is very stern. "My good man [friend]," he says, with a bite in his voice, "how did you manage to get in here, no better dressed than you are?" The man has no excuse. He is speechless.

(c) Deciding which text to study

The text of this parable is somewhat uncertain, since only Matthew has recorded it, and he spliced it together with his version of the Banquet parable at that. Most recent studies concur in the above reconstruction.

(d) Meaning in the setting of Jesus' life

Matthew obviously understood this parable as an allegorical depiction of the final judgment. The king is God, the son Jesus, the improperly dressed guest someone who joined the church without undergoing repentance. On the day of judgment faithless Christians will be singled out by God and cast "into outer darkness." In Matthew's eyes the parable was a stern warning to Christian converts not to enter the church under false pretenses.

When Jesus taught, however, the church did not yet exist. He spoke rather in the context of the movement of healing and repentance that he (and John the Baptist before him) had awakened among the "poor" (the disaffiliated outsiders to establishment Judaism). The "righteous," more religious Jews were looking down on this movement.

Jesus saw in this awakening to new life the advent of the kingdom of God. Why could not the Jewish establishment see it too? Why were they so critical and half-hearted toward what was happening? They had better watch out lest, like a guest with shabby clothes at a king's wedding, they are "thrown out." In this moment of joyous revival and repentance among "sinners" it disturbed Jesus that the Jewish leaders were responding so inappropriately.

30. THE SERVANT ENTRUSTED WITH SUPERVISION (Matt. 24:45–51/Luke 12:42–46)

(a) Getting oriented

The servant in this parable behaved very badly, thinking his master was not due back from his journey for some time yet. This is clearly another instance of "self-defeating" action.

(b) Getting acquainted with the texts

The texts are remarkably similar:

Matthew 24:45–51	Luke 12:42–46
Who then is the faithful and wise servant, whom his master has set over his household, to give them their food at the proper time?	Who then is the faithful and wise steward, whom his master will set over his household to give them their portion of food at the proper time?
Blessed is that servant whom his master when he comes will find so doing.	Blessed is that servant whom his master when he comes will find so doing.
Truly, I say to you, he will set him over all his possessions. But if that wicked servant says to himself, "My master is delayed," and begins to beat his fellow servants, and eats and drinks with the drunken, the master of that servant will come on a day when he does not expect him and at an hour he does not know, and will punish him, and put him with the hypocrites; there men will weep and gnash their teeth.	Truly I tell you, he will set him over all his possessions. But if that servant says to himself, "My master is delayed," and begins to beat the manservants and the maid-servants, and to eat and drink and get drunk, the master of that servant will come on a day when he does not expect him and at an hour he does not know, and will punish him, and put him with the unfaithful.

Matthew and Luke seem to be copying this parable, word for word, from a common source, and yet there are a few minor variations. At the very beginning Luke speaks of a "steward" who had under him "menservants and maidservants." But later on the steward is called a "servant" (slave). Matthew's version is more consistent at this point. His leading figure is throughout a "servant" (slave) who has been given *temporary* charge over the other household slaves while the master is away on a journey.

On the other hand Matthew has changed and expanded the ending of the parable. Luke's version stays within the boundaries of an ordinary story. When the master returns and finds the slave, in whom he had placed so much confidence, abusing that trust, he punishes and demotes him. Matthew interprets this allegorically as a reference to punishment that will be meted out in the *afterlife* to "hypocrites," and adds a sentence that we saw previously (in our discussion of the Guest without a Wedding Garment) that is peculiar to his Gospel ("There men will weep and gnash their teeth").

(c) Deciding which text to study

The previous discussion would suggest that we should use Matthew's version of this parable if we wish to study it in its most original form, but without Matthew's final phrases (everything after "and will punish him").

(d) Meaning in the setting of Jesus' life

The setting in their Gospels to which both Matthew and Luke assigned this parable indicates that they understood it as an allegory depicting the coming of the Son of man "at an hour you do not expect" (Matt. 24:44/Luke 12:40). Read in this light, the master would be Jesus who has gone away (into heaven) and put responsibility for his household (the church) in the hands of his disciple-apostles. Those apostolic leaders who do not exercise a good "stewardship" (Luke) over the church will be punished when the Lord returns.

This way of understanding the parable is meaningful but not what it meant when Jesus first told it. The servant who took advantage of his position of authority over the other servants would have reminded *Jesus'* audiences of the scribes or the Pharisees to whom (it was thought) had been given power to open and shut "the kingdom of heaven" (Matt. 23:13/Luke 11:52). Elsewhere in the Gospels we hear Jesus charging these leaders with having abused their fellow Jews by having taken "away the key of knowledge" (Luke 11:52). They "shut the kingdom of heaven against men," he said, for they neither entered themselves, nor allowed "those who would enter to go in" (Matt. 23:13), all the while enjoying the privileged benefits of their authority over others. A time of reckoning was at hand.

This is another one of Jesus' many words of warning to the leaders of the Jewish establishment.

31. THE WICKED TENANT FARMERS
(Mark 12:1–11/Matt. 21:33–43
Luke 20:9–18/Thomas 65)

(a) Getting oriented

This parable brings to a climax the parables of self-defeating rejection we have been studying. For the first time we read not only of people who criticize, or fumble their opportunity, or beat and abuse others, but of men who are prepared to murder to gain their ends.

(b) Getting acquainted with the texts

The three synoptic texts of this parable each differ from the others at significant points, and together form a striking contrast to the much simpler version in Thomas.

Here is another instance where a parable has been expanded and reshaped into an allegory. The differences, for example, between Matthew's version of this story and Luke's are strikingly similar to those previously noted in the case of their respective versions of the parable of the Banquet. Here, as there, Matthew speaks of "servants" whereas Luke mentions only a single "servant" (as in Mark and Thomas). In Matthew and Mark the vineyard is described (in the opening verses) in a way that reminds the reader of the classic allegory in Isaiah where Israel is said to be God's vineyard (Isa. 5:1ff.). This allegorical flourish is missing in Luke and Thomas. But all three synoptic accounts (in contrast to Thomas) shape the story into an allegory of holy history. The tenants are the Jews to whom God sends servants (the prophets), and finally his "beloved son" (Mark, Luke). The son's execution outside the vineyard (Jesus' crucifixion outside Jerusalem) leads to the destruction of the original tenants (the destruction of Jerusalem) and transfer of the property to "others" (the Christian church). Only one important feature of early Christian faith could not be brought into this story: Jesus' resurrection. But this was added through the attached saying about the "stone which the builders rejected" becoming "the head of the corner."

It would go beyond the limits of our present study to discuss in detail the way each of the synoptic versions developed this allegory. It is sufficient for our purposes simply to note that originally the story was a much simpler one. Scholars suspected this long before the publication of the Gospel of Thomas. With the appearance of this Gospel, these suspicions have now been remarkably confirmed, for all the allegorical flourishes are missing from the Thomas text. Instead we have a rather straightforward story about a "good man" who rented out his vineyard to husbandmen. In the course of time these tenants tried to take it over for themselves. After beating up two messengers sent to collect the rent, they murdered the owner's son. Since the son was the heir, the property could now fall into their hands.

This episode (strange as it might sound) fits well into the contemporary social situation in Palestine. A great deal of Palestinian property in Jesus' time was owned by absentee landlords. When the titleholders of this property died and there were no heirs, it could be taken over by those who were working it. The story implies that this is what the men in this story have in mind. Seeing the owner's son arriving (after they had beaten up the previous two servants), they may have thought that the owner himself was dead and that the son was coming to take up his inheritance. By killing him, they could get the vineyard for themselves.

(c) Deciding which text to study

The Thomas version of this parable is the simplest and probably the most original. If we wish to use a canonical version, Luke's ac-

Matt. 21:33-43	Mark 12:1-11	Luke 20:9-18	Thomas 65
There was a householder who planted a vineyard, and set a hedge around it, and dug it, and built a tower, and let it out to tenants, and went into another country. When the season of fruit drew near, he sent his servants to the tenants to get his fruit; and the tenants took his servants and beat one, killed another, and stoned another. Again he sent other servants, more than the first; and they did the same to them. Afterward he sent his son to them, saying, "They will respect my son." But when the tenants saw the son, they said to themselves, "This is the heir; come,	A man planted a vineyard, and set a hedge around it, and dug a pit for the wine press, and built a tower, and let it out to tenants, and went into another country. When the time came, he sent a servant to the tenants, to get from them some of the fruit of the vineyard. And they took him and beat him, and sent him away empty-handed. Again he sent to them another servant, and they wounded him in the head, and treated him shamefully. And he sent another, and him they killed; and so with many others, some they beat and some they killed. He had still one other, a beloved son; finally he sent him to them, saying, "They will respect my son." But those tenants said to one	A man planted a vineyard, and let it out to tenants, and went into another country for a long while. When the time came, he sent a servant to the tenants, that they should give him some of the fruit of the vineyard; but the tenants beat him and sent him away empty-handed. Again he sent another servant; him also they beat and treated shamefully, and sent him away empty-handed. And he sent yet a third; this one they wounded and cast out. Then the owner of the vineyard said, "What shall I do? I will send my beloved son; it may be they will respect him." But when the tenants saw him, they said to themselves, "This is the heir; let us kill him, that the inheritance	A good man had a vineyard. He gave it to husbandmen that they might work it, and he received its fruit at their hand. He sent his servant, that the husbandmen might give him the fruit of the vineyard. They seized his servant, they beat him; and all but killed him. The servant came [and] told his master. His master said: Perhaps they did not know him. He sent another servant; the husbandmen beat the other also. Then the master sent his son. He said: Perhaps they will reverence my son. Those husbandmen, since they knew that he was the heir of the vineyard, they seized him [and]

let us kill him and have his in- heritance."

And they took him and cast him out of the vineyard, and killed him. When therefore the owner of the vineyard comes, what will he do to those ten- ants? They said to him, "He will put those wretches to a miser- able death, and let out the vine- yard to other tenants who will give him the fruits in their sea- sons." Jesus said to them, "Have you never read in the scriptures: 'The very stone which the builders rejected has become the head of the corner; this was the Lord's doing, and it is marvelous in our eyes'? Therefore I tell you, the king- dom of God will be taken away from you and given to a nation producing the fruits of it."

another, "This is the heir; come, let us kill him, and the inheri- tance will be ours." And they took him and killed him and cast him out of the vineyard. What will the owner of the vine- yard do?

He will come and destroy the tenants, and give the vineyard to others.

Have you not read the scrip- tures: "The very stone which the builders rejected has become the head of the corner; this was the Lord's doing, and it is mar- velous in our eyes'"?

may be ours." And they cast him out of the vineyard and killed him. What then will the owner of the vineyard do to them? He will come and destroy those tenants, and give the vine- yard to others.

When they heard this, they said, "God forbid!" But he looked at them and said, "What then is this that is written: 'The very stone which the builders reject- ed has become the head of the corner'?

Every one who falls on that stone will be broken to pieces; but when it falls on any one it will crush him."

killed him. He that hath ears, let him hear.

count would be the next best. If Luke's text is chosen for study, it might be well to simplify it through comparison with Thomas, so that its allegorical flourishes are kept at a minimum.

(d) Meaning in the setting of Jesus' life

If Jesus did tell this parable approximately as Thomas tells it, it is certainly not hard to imagine its original reference. In the parables studied previously in this chapter we can sense the rising tide of opposition against Jesus. The Jewish leaders are not only turning a deaf ear. They are more and more opposing Jesus with criticism and mounting rejection. Bitter hostility is in the air. Murder is not out of the question. The Jewish establishment is acting like lawless tenant farmers who simply will not respond to the absentee owner when he sends for the rent. Yes, they are even prepared to murder the owner's son to gain their ends. Jesus is warning the Jewish leaders not to pursue their rejection of what God is doing among them to its bitter end.

(e) Listening to the parables today

Do not forget to memorize and retell these parables. Then share freely the thoughts and emotions they arouse. What follows are simply examples of the kinds of things I think of as I study these stories.

The complacency of the upper classes (spoken of in the previous chapter) is seldom a point of stability. The pressures of history keep building. No one can remain an island of indecision for very long. Life has a way of throwing us off balance. Again and again we are forced to decide. This is our highest dignity. It also can lead to our greatest tragedies.

As the pressures mount, our response will be wise or foolish, right or wrong, self-defeating or meaningful. The moral philosophers of our time often speak of areas of gray. They shrink from blacks and whites. All actions, they say, are ambivalent, woven of good and evil.

But in the parables we have been looking at people act foolishly. It is not a question of gray. They really do mess things up. Like petulant children, grumbling at their playmates, like silly girls at a wedding, like a shabbily dressed guest at a gala social affair, the powerful fail to grasp the challenge before them. Their initial indecision turns to abuse, hostility and murder. We destroy that which threatens us. The Jewish establishment was getting ready to destroy Jesus.

It happens again and again. Those in power despise those who threaten that power. Those in power begin feeling they are right. They cannot take opposition. If the opposition is weak, they may ignore it for a time. But as it mounts they counterattack.

History will not stand still. Love keeps on battering away at all narrow notions of privilege and righteousness. The egotism that power breeds must topple and fall in the face of more compassionate ways. Especially since the time of Jesus we are increasingly confident that love will eventually conquer the earth. It is written into the fabric of the universe. It is grounded in the nature of God. But on the way to this goal there is struggle.

Where is this conflict at work today? Self-righteousness is still a deadly force in the life of the world. Perhaps more than anything else it still divides people against each other and inflames their hostile passions. Also the world-wide disparities between rich and poor must again be mentioned in this connection. Hunger stalks the globe while some overeat and exhaust the world's resources in extravagant living. A key question for our generation is the response that will be made to all this, especially on the part of the wealthy, righteous, Christianized West. If we do not say yes to compassion, will we eventually say no? Will our hearts harden into criticism? Priding ourselves that all is in order, perhaps too late we will learn that we are "empty," ready targets for invasion by inhuman demons. Half-hearted efforts will only land us in the embarrassing circumstance of the guest at a wedding banquet in dirty clothes. While the world goes hungry we will be found eating and drinking and beating up our fellow servants. Yes, we might even murder those messengers who bring us the bad news that we are in fact not as "righteous" as we think we are (remember Martin Luther King?).

It is a fateful moment for establishment Christianity. But that is the way things go, because that is the way man is: never secure, always poised for fresh adventure, free to move in one direction or another. The parables we have just studied keep on warning us against taking a "way that leads to death."

IX. MEANINGFUL ACTION

32. GOING BEFORE THE JUDGE
(Matt. 5:25f./Luke 12:57–59)

(a) Getting oriented

We are nearing the close of our study. A final group of parables remains. They are mostly short and to the point. And they all portray action of a meaningful kind. Here again are people confronted by crisis situations. Some of the crises are heavy with danger. Others are alive with joy. In each case, not to act would be tragic. These parables show us how people should act when confronted by God's gracious presence and call to newness of life.

(b) Getting acquainted with the text

The two versions of this parable in Matthew and Luke are quite similar, but the settings are different.

Matthew 5:25–26	Luke 12:57–59
Make friends quickly with your accuser, while you are going with him to court, lest your accuser *hand you over* to the judge, and the judge to the guard, and you be put in prison; truly, I say to you,	And why do you not judge for yourselves what is right? As you go with your accuser before the magistrate, make an effort to settle with him on the way, lest he *drag* you to the judge, and the judge

you will never get out till you have paid the last penny.

hand you over to the officer, and the officer put you in prison. I tell you, you will never get out till you have paid the very last copper.

The picture is that of a debtor being dragged (Luke) into court by a creditor to whom he owes money. Jewish law says nothing about throwing a person into prison for nonpayment of debt. Indeed Jewish law says nothing at all about imprisonment. Jesus is therefore referring to Roman legal practices that his Jewish audience would no doubt consider barbarous.

The slight shift in terminology for the officials involved ("judge" in Matthew, "magistrate" in Luke) reflects the differences between Jewish and Roman judicial terms. Matthew's account is the more Jewish. Both accounts stress how important it is that the accused should not delay, but settle with his accuser while on the way to court, lest the judgment turn out against him and he be thrown into prison, and there have to pay every last penny (copper).

(c) Deciding which text to study

In this instance, although the texts differ somewhat, the variations are not significant. Either text will do.

(d) Meaning in the setting of Jesus' life

Matthew adds this parable to a section of the Sermon on the Mount where anger against a brother is the topic. For him, apparently, it is not so much a parable as a straightforward admonition. When accused, one should avoid angry outbursts and settle accounts as quickly as possible.

In Luke, however, this teaching stands in a quite different setting. There it follows a warning to the multitudes to open their eyes and learn how to "interpret the present time." Luke obviously sees here more than practical advice about handling accusations. A man dragged by his accuser into debt-court is a picture for him of those who are confronted by the presence of the "kingdom." Judaism is being summoned to repentance. If it does not make room for compassion toward its ostracized classes, it will perish. It is time for decisive action. "Settle now with the challenges facing you, and don't wait until it's too late." "Judge for yourselves what is appropriate" (Luke). Act as a man would act who is being dragged by his creditor into court.

As to the relevance of this parable for our time, see our comments at the end of this chapter.

33. THE DISHONEST STEWARD (Luke 16:1–8a)

(a) Getting oriented

Like the crisis spoken of in the previous parable, this one too has to do with money. Only in this instance the man involved is not in debt. He is in difficulty because of the sloppy way he managed the business entrusted to him. Faced with impending dismissal from his job, he formulates a plan of action and carries it out with great cunning.

(b) Getting acquainted with the text

The text of the parable itself appears to be flawless. The problem in this instance is knowing which of the string of attached sayings (vv. 8–13) belongs to the story in its original setting. They give the appearance of "notes for three separate sermons on the parable as text" (Dodd).

If any of these attached sayings provides a key to the original meaning of this parable, it would be the first one: "The master commended the dishonest steward for his prudence" (v. 8a). By "the master" here is probably not meant the rich man in the parable (whose steward was so incompetent and treated him so badly), but Jesus. The same expression (translated "the Lord") is also found at the conclusion of the parable of the Unjust Judge (Luke 18:6). Here as there it would appear that the tradition has preserved a comment by Jesus himself on his own parable. And what "the master" said in this instance is that this devious steward acted commendably in doing what he did.

What did he actually do?

> There was a rich man who had a steward, and charges were brought to him that this man was wasting his goods.
>
> And he called him and said to him, "What is this that I hear about you? Turn in the account of your stewardship, for you can no longer be steward."
>
> And the steward said to himself, "What shall I do, since my master is taking the stewardship away from me? I am not strong enough to dig, and I am ashamed to beg. I have decided what to do, so that people may receive me into their houses when I am put out of the stewardship."
>
> So, summoning his master's debtors one by one, he said to the first, "How much do you owe my master?" He said, "A hundred measures of oil." And he said to him, "Take your bill, and sit down quickly and write fifty." Then he said to another, "And how much do you owe?" He said, "A hundred measures of wheat." He said to him, "Take your bill, and write eighty."
>
> The master [Jesus] commended the dishonest steward for his prudence.

There are some striking parallels between this parable and the parable of the Wicked Judge. Both parables make us smile a bit, especially as we listen to their central characters muse to themselves about their predicament and calculate what they shall do about it. In both cases too (as just noted) Jesus comments on the parabolic significance of the actions decided upon.

In this instance the story itself is plain enough. The manager of a sizeable farming operation is charged with wasting his master's goods. The charges must be true, for the poor fellow makes no effort to defend or explain himself when the manager fires him. Instead, recognizing that he is out of shape physically ("not strong enough to dig"), and too proud to beg, he devises a plan to ingratiate himself with those with whom he has been doing business.

He calls in his master's debtors and asks them how much they owe (another indication perhaps of how badly he was managing. *He* doesn't know!). "A hundred measures of oil," one of them says, or about 800 gallons, the yield of 146 olive trees (Jeremias). "A hundred measures of wheat," says another, roughly the yield of 100 acres. The sums owed are enormous, the debt reductions large. Obviously this "dishonest steward" was totally unscrupulous. He defrauded his employer right and left.

And yet, as with the Wicked Judge, there was something good about this scoundrel. "The master commended the dishonest steward for his prudence." Like the maidens waiting for the coming of the bridegroom who carried an extra flask of oil (Matt. 25:4), and the servant who took care of the household while his master went away on a journey (Matt. 24:45/Luke 12:42), this man was "wise." He sized up the situation accurately and acted accordingly.

(c) Deciding which text to study

The parable itself (as Luke records it) presents no serious problems. We can take it as it is. Also, the first of several attached sayings may be original ("The master commended the dishonest steward for his prudence"). The sayings that follow are less likely so. The words may be words of Jesus, but they were not originally spoken in this context.

(d) Meaning in the setting of Jesus' life

Joachim Jeremias suggests that the story of the Dishonest Steward could have been based on an actual incident. In an irresponsible farm manager (about whom there may have been a good bit of malicious gossip) Jesus saw something to commend. It was the cunning way he dealt with a personal crisis and acted to save his neck.

Luke may give us a hint as to the original point of this parable by having placed it right after three parables told by Jesus in defense of his table fellowship with "sinners" (The Lost Sheep, Coin, Son). In those three parables (as noted earlier) Jesus points to the joy of "heaven" over the restoration of that which is lost, and challenges

his Pharisaic critics as to the adequacy of their charity toward alienated Jewish brothers and sisters.

For Jesus this drying up of compassion among the Jewish leaders for those who are weak and sinful was a crisis. If unresolved, it
could lead to the splintering and disintegration of Jewish society.
Even more, it was tantamount to a rejection of God who loves both
righteous and sinner alike (Matt. 5:45).

Would that these leaders had the "wisdom" of this dishonest
steward! Would that they could discern the challenge confronting
them and take just as decisive steps to secure their future!

34. THE TREASURE (Matt. 13:44/Thomas 109)

(a) Getting oriented

Two of the shortest parables that Jesus told (the Treasure and
the Pearl) are about men acting in response to unexpected discoveries of great value. In both instances the actions taken are exactly
what's called for.

(b) Getting acquainted with the texts

The Thomas version of this parable is so different that it can
hardly be compared to the version in Matthew. It is interesting primarily as a contrast.

Matthew 13:44	Thomas 109
The kingdom of heaven is like treasure hidden in a field, which a man found and covered up; then in his joy he goes and sells all that he has and buys that field.	The Kingdom is like a man who had in his field a [hidden] treasure about which he did not know; and [after] he died, he left it to his [son. The] son also did not know; he took [possession of] the field and sold it. The man who bought it came to plough and [found] the treasure. He began to lend money at interest to whomever he chose.

In Thomas the man buys the field in which lies the treasure (after it had been passed from father to son), then discovers it (no doubt to the chagrin of the man who sold it to him). It is just the opposite in Matthew's account. There the treasure is discovered and then the field is bought. Thomas tells us how the treasure was discovered. This fortunate fellow was ploughing (perhaps he was a hired hand of the field's owner). In Palestine in Jesus' time silver coins and jewels deposited in a jar were frequently buried in the ground for safekeeping. There is a touch of humor in Matthew's account of how this man hastily covered his discovery up again and then "in his joy" went about obtaining the field. It may be true that his action was legal (Jeremias), but it was hardly moral! Nevertheless here was the chance of a lifetime!

(c) Deciding which text to study

The longer Thomas version complicates and subverts the plot line of this story. Matthew's text is by far the preferable one (although Thomas supplements the canonical version by making explicit that the treasure was discovered while ploughing).

(d) Meaning in the setting of Jesus' life

Matthew's Gospel locates this parable among those that were initially spoken to "disciples" (Matt. 13:36). In this instance he might well be right, for it strikes a very positive note. It invites those who hear it to let the joy of a new discovery motivate them, as it did this poor hired man. Through this parable Jesus seems to be reaching out to those who are experiencing what he experienced: that God is already working to heal and to save. The kingdom of God is already manifesting itself (in advance of its apocalyptic manifestation). Those who "discover" this great reality should not hesitate. "Let the *joy* of your newfound awareness of God's grace move and motivate you as did that of a hired man who accidently found buried treasure and sold all that he had to buy the field where it lay."

35. THE PEARL (Matt. 13:45f./Thomas 76)

(a) Getting oriented

Like the parable of the Treasure, so here too a man "finds-sells-buys" out of sheer exuberance over what he has discovered.

(b) Getting acquainted with the texts

The text of this parable in Thomas is of more than ordinary interest. Joachim Jeremias argues that it may in fact be the more original version.

Matthew 13:45f.	Thomas 76
The kingdom of heaven is like a merchant in search of fine pearls, who on finding one pearl of great value, went and sold all that he had and bought it.	The Kingdom of the Father is like a merchant, who had a load [of goods] and found a pearl. That merchant was wise. He sold the load, and bought for himself the pearl alone.

In both Matthew and Thomas the story has to do with merchants who discover an exquisite pearl, the equivalent in antiquity to a valuable diamond in today's market.

The main difference in the two versions is that in Thomas the merchant is a *general* merchandiser, while in Matthew he is a *pearl* merchant "in search of fine pearls." The element of surprise and good fortune at finding such a valuable pearl is thereby heightened in Thomas. The man was not looking for pearls (as in Matthew). He was simply a buyer and seller of goods. But in the course of his commercial enterprises he chanced upon this exceptional pearl and at once recognized its worth. He did not hesitate. Like the man who discovered buried treasure, he sensed immediately that this was the chance of a lifetime. He sold out his total inventory in order to buy this one small but enormously valuable jewel.

(c) Deciding which text to study

Both versions describe a merchant's once-in-a-lifetime discovery and his response. The drama of the story is slightly heightened in

Thomas, where the merchant is a dealer in general goods rather than a pearl merchant. This might be the more original form of the story.

(d) Meaning in the setting of Jesus' life

When "God" (God's kingdom) suddenly becomes real to you (Jesus seems to be saying) let the joy of this discovery move you to action. Be like the man who stumbled upon a pearl of great value and sold everything to buy it.

36. THE TOWER BUILDER AND THE KING
(Luke 14:28–32)

(a) Getting oriented

God's presence awakens action—spontaneous, wholehearted, joyful action. But *intelligent* action as well. This seems to be the message of the Tower Builder and the King Contemplating War. These two parables are so tightly linked in both form and content that we shall treat them as one.

(b) Getting acquainted with the text

Only Luke has preserved the texts of these parabolic episodes.

Which of you desiring to build a tower, does not first sit down and count the cost, whether he has enough to complete it? Otherwise, when he has laid a foundation, and is not able to finish, all who see it begin to mock him, saying, "This man began to build, and was not able to finish."

Or what king, going to encounter another king in war, will not sit down first and take counsel whether he is able with ten thousand to meet him who comes against him with twenty thousand? And if not, while the other is yet a great way off, he sends an embassy and asks terms of peace.

It should be noted first of all that both parables are framed as questions anticipating decisive answers. "Can you imagine a builder, a king acting otherwise than described? Certainly not!" The structure involved in the first picture could be a "farm building" rather than a "tower" (Jeremias). In either case, the building contemplated is a sizeable one, requiring careful assessment of resources for completing it. A king going to war must do the same. If not, the building may never be finished (to the embarrassment of its owner), and the king may go down in defeat.

(c) Deciding which text to use

The only problem here is whether to translate "tower" or "farm building," a minor issue indeed!

(d) Meaning in the setting of Jesus' life

In Luke these little parables are sandwiched between sayings of Jesus that speak of radical discipleship.

> If any one comes to me and does not hate his own father and mother and wife and children and brothers and sisters, yes, and even his own life, he cannot be my disciple. Whoever does not bear his own cross and come after me, cannot be my disciple . . . (Luke 14:26–27).
> So therefore, whoever of you does not renounce all that he has cannot be my disciple (Luke 14:33).

These words suggest that the advent of God's kingdom upsets everything and calls for a total response. They remind us of the actions of the men in the parables of the Pearl and the Hidden Treasure.

But in advocating such a total response to God's initiative, Jesus by no means meant to say that one should act thoughtlessly. It is well to look ahead. It is appropriate to think about weighty actions beforehand to make sure that what is undertaken can be brought to a good conclusion.

Many of the parables we have studied appear to have been addressed to Jesus' opponents. These final parabolic questions might well have been spoken to his friends. They portray people on the brink of great enterprises. Such is the situation of those about to respond to the revelation of God's love. It is an awesome undertaking. A prospective disciple might well pause before launching out on a journey of this magnitude and count the cost.

(e) Listening to the parables today

What I hear Jesus calling for in these parables is not a mighty effort of the will. It is not as though he were saying in some vague, generalized sense: Be good, be compassionate, be more loving. He is pointing us rather to how people do in fact act when faced by concrete unexpected discoveries and challenges.

Life is not a vacuum in which I stand alone with my will and my efforts. Life is a ceaseless flow of surprising events and ordeals. And there, hidden in the midst of it, is that gracious power we call God.

What is decisive is how we respond to this "flow" of events. What is decisive is how we answer the many moments of decision thrust upon us. What is decisive is whether we say "yes," whether we open ourselves to them, whether we greet them wholeheartedly with our whole being, our body, our emotions, our intelligence.

When the merchant discovered that marvelous pearl, no one needed to tell him what to do. No one needed to say, you must feel joyful about this discovery, you must sell all that you have to buy it. Rather, because this man was free enough and mature enough to size up the situation and act, he just knew what he must do. The same is true of every one of the figures in the parables we have just studied. Even the man who contemplates erecting a fine farm building, and the king getting ready for a major battle, in their moments of reflection, are showing the qualities that Jesus admired. They were deep in thought, profoundly engaged with the challenges before them.

What is called for then is not so much an unnatural intensification of will, as alertness, openness to the moment, and to God in the moment, and readiness to act with the totality of our powers (emotional and mental).

Again I think (as I listen to these parables) of the great issues confronting our globe: self-righteousness, loneliness, urban decay, world hunger, and the like. But I also think of all those moments in the course of a day or week when I am confronted by the "voice" of God. *Reading these parables encourages me to be more myself in these situations, more attentive to the total response called for and already rising within me.* They make me want to live my life more fully alive to God and to history.

QUESTIONS FOR DISCUSSION
AND FURTHER STUDY:

1. When was the last time you were face to face with a big decision?
2. How would you characterize your response (like that of the merchant or the builder)?
3. Do you recall ever responding to a "discovery" in the spiritual realm in a manner similar to the man who discovered treasure? Why did you? Why don't you do so more often?

CONCLUDING COMMENTS

Having finished looking at each of the previous thirty-six parables, the worst mistake we could make is to think that now we are finished. As I have repeatedly suggested, we cannot fully appropriate these stories until we have memorized them and can retell them as easily as we tell our favorite anecdote. In spite of repeated encouragement I suspect it will be the rare student or study group that will conclude a first study of these stories with that achievement securely behind them.

Even after memorizing these stories, we will need to hear them again and again, both in their original setting and today. Unless they become dynamic memories, easily brought to consciousness, they will fade within us in favor of other models and modes of thought.

I believe a foremost pedagogical and spiritual task before the church, if it wishes to maintain its vital contact with the mind of Jesus, is just such a deliberate effort at opening itself to the parabolic treasures of the Gospels. Mastery at this point will require study and restudy of the stories just surveyed.

I cannot claim myself to be more than a novice at this task. What is offered on the previous pages is no more than a tool for getting started. But even with this much behind us, it might be well to pause and try to identify at least some of the learning that has already taken place. Here again each student will have a different story to tell. What I share at this point is only one man's musings, set down as a stimulant to others.

1. Through this study my image of Jesus has undergone a subtle but significant shift. Even though a teacher myself, I had never thought before as much as I have in working with this material about his artfulness as teacher. Here is a man of deep concerns, with a passion to communicate, but he did not hammer away. Rather he clothed his concerns in stories that showed the profoundest respect for the intelligence of his audience. Jesus spoke on one occasion of casting out demons by God's gentle power ("the finger of God"). The same could be said of his approach to teaching. Not harsh harangue, but gentle, sometimes humorous, sometimes biting image and winsome evocation consistently characterize his effort at counteracting what he felt to be destructive tendencies in the spirit of his time.

2. In the parables, perhaps as nowhere else, we can get a feeling for the priorities of Jesus' concerns. By taking the stories as a whole one begins to sense where the real weight of his thinking lay, where its focal centers were—the points to which it returned again and again. These can be summarized very simply. He felt the world to be radiant with the gracious, forgiving, healing activity of God. It was a disaster to him that the people of his time, the leaders especially, were so hostile to those who were most alienated and therefore most in need of this God. He felt that the "religious" just had to face up to what they were doing, and that they were indeed capable of doing so. The active goodness of God, the summons to faith, to compassion and love, and the urgency that men and women do something about their most obvious responsibilities toward each other— these are the notes that sound again and again through the stories we have just studied.

3. One theme above all, however, surfaces in these parables: the inherent dangers of self-righteousness, the supreme worth of humble repentance. To a too-reverent seeker who had called him good Jesus once replied: *"Why do you call me good? No one is good but God alone"* (Mark 10:18). In parable after parable he says the same thing. Surely Jesus is the humblest of world religious leaders. It is dangerous, yes fatal, he insists, not to face up to our fallibility and sin and learn to forgive and be forgiven.

4. Surprising is the simplicity and down-to-earthness of the stories that Jesus fashioned to convey this message. They testify to the

way his mind dwelt on the ordinary. If Jesus did speak of an apocalyptic future, a time when God would shatter the fabric of history, and introduce a totally new world, one must say that this was not by any means what preoccupied him. What preoccupied him, the parables would suggest, was the interrelationship of the ordinary and the spiritual. The goodness of God became manifest to him in the bumbling response of a friend at midnight, and the kingdom of God in the everyday miracle of leaven in dough. The profoundest issues of life were forcefully displayed by two men in prayer, and how a man should act could be seen in a scoundrel scrambling for a place for himself in the wake of precipitous dismissal from his job. That we are surprised by this down-to-earthness of his teaching testifies no doubt to the plastic image of Jesus that has been too long dominant in Christendom.

I look forward to a lifelong pondering of these stories. I look forward to the way this process might help me be what the parables speak of: more aware of God, more forgiving, more compassionate, more decisive, more able to see the world of ordinary events alive with the reality of God's kingdom, content to be a part of the coming of that kingdom in whatever way God's "gentle" power makes possible.

SUGGESTIONS FOR GROUP STUDY

A. In approaching the study of a given parable it is imperative that the group read and discuss the scriptural text (or texts) of the parable *before* reading the observations given in the manual. In other words, the study group should itself look at the text, study it, and make its own observations first. To facilitate this, I have found it helpful to duplicate the texts of the parables to be studied, so that they appear by themselves on a sheet of paper that can be circulated to each member of the study group and used as a worksheet. I usually then make some rather specific study suggestions like: "Underscore the words (on the worksheet) in Luke's version of the parable of the Lost Sheep that do not appear in Matthew." Or: "Circle the words in Luke's version that are different from those in Matthew." This kind of exercise encourages careful textual observation, often leads to a discussion of the differences between the texts, and lays the groundwork for the entire subsequent study. Getting acquainted with the texts is the most important single step in parables study.

B. After determining which text to study, be sure to take time to memorize the parable well enough to retell it from memory. I sometimes do this by breaking the study group into pairs, with each person in the pair telling the parable to the other. I emphasize that they should keep practicing until they can tell the parable easily and with appropriate emotion. Then I have the group reassemble and ask for volunteers who will tell the parable to the whole group. This exercise of telling the parables is very important. It is not enough simply to read a parable. We should have them stored up in our memories, so that we can hear them over and over again as parables in their own right.

C. Be sure the group understands what the parable meant (insofar as this can be determined) in the time of Jesus. This alone will provide a control over too much contemporary allegorizing, a continuing danger and problem in parable interpretation. When this happens, the parable does not speak to us; we simply pour our own thoughts into the parable.

But with that point established, the group should then spend time just sharing what thoughts arise within them as they listen to the story today. A parable starts us thinking. It is not meant to deliver a finished idea so much as awaken a train of reflection. The sharing and exploration of these reflections will be one of the more important phases of the study process. We want to study the parables not as museum pieces but as living contemporary words.

D. In general this study manual should be used as a supplement and check, not as a crutch. As indicated in point A above, the students should themselves study the texts before looking at commentaries. The same would hold true for "deciding which text to study" and "listening to the parables today." Determining the meaning of a given parable in the setting of Jesus' life does require the help of a manual of this kind, but no one has the final word on the contemporary meaning of these stories. If you find yourself disagreeing with my comments at any point, you might be right, or we both might be wrong. It is the nature of a parable to launch us on a search that keeps on opening up into new territory.

ANNOTATED BIBLIOGRAPHY

The following list is far from exhaustive. The study of Jesus' parables is one of the most rapidly expanding fields in contemporary Biblical study. For a comprehensive bibliography, see John Dominic Crossan, "A Basic Bibliography for Parables Research," in *Semeia* 1, 1974, pp. 236–274, and Warren S. Kissinger, *The Parables of Jesus: A History of Interpretation and Bibliography,* The Scarecrow Press, 1979. I cite here only the more substantial recent book-length studies, as well as a few background works that might be useful to the beginning student.

Armstrong, Edward. *The Gospel Parables,* Sheed and Ward, 1967.
    Based squarely on the work of Dodd and Jeremias (see below), this work goes beyond them in exploring the contemporary relevance of the parables. Some sixty parables and similes are discussed, including several from John's Gospel. The author is Vicar of St. Mark's Church, Cambridge, England.

Barclay, William. *And Jesus Said,* The Saint Andrew Press, 1970.
    This is a reprint of a study first published in 1952 by the foremost expositor of the New Testament for lay people. The author writes in a simple style about the meaning of thirty-three parables. The main emphasis is on their relevance for today, but there are helpful comments as well about their original significance. Designed initially for Bible class use.

Barclay, William. *The Gospels & Acts,* Vol. One, SCM, 1976.
    A fascinating, detailed, yet popularly written account of how Matthew, Mark and Luke came to be written. An excellent *background* discussion for a study of the parables.

Barrett, C. K. *The New Testament Background: Selected Documents,* Harper & Row, 1961.
    A valuable collection of first-century documents illuminating the world in which Jesus lived and taught.

Beare, Frank. *The Earliest Records of Jesus,* Abingdon, 1962.
    Here is an astute running commentary on the parallel versions of the first three Gospels, as arranged in *Gospel Parallels,* edited by Throckmorton (see below). Useful for the advanced student of these Gospels. Beare is Professor of N. T. Studies at Trinity College, Toronto.

Carlston, Charles E. *The Parables of the Triple Tradition,* Fortress Press, 1975.
    A most careful scholarly study of those parables that occur in all three of the synoptic Gospels, with attention both to their meaning in the life of Jesus and the use to which they were put at each stage of the tradition. An important work for advanced study of the parables.

Crossan, John Dominic. *In Parables,* Harper & Row, 1973.
    A study that breaks new ground in appreciating "metaphor" as a mode of communication. There are some very helpful textual observations here as well. But the author goes too far at points in pressing all the parables into a single mold and explaining them in existential terms.

Dodd, C. H. *The Parables of the Kingdom,* rev. ed., Charles Scribner's Sons, 1961.
    A book that paved the way for the modern consensus in parables study by looking at them, for the first time, with rigorous attention to their original setting in the life of Jesus, and

especially in the context of his proclamation of the kingdom of God.

Flood, Edmund. *Parables of Jesus,* Paulist Press, 1970.
   A very simple, clearly written analysis of twelve parables by a noted Catholic scholar, bringing out both their original meaning and contemporary relevance.

Granskou, David. *Preaching on the Parables,* Fortress Press, 1972.
   Contains an excellent description of the history of parable interpretation, as well as brief and often pithy comments on thirty-one parables. The author emphasizes the humor of many of these stories as well as their prophetic impact.

Hargreaves, John. *A Guide to the Parables,* S.P.C.K., 1968.
   This booklet is especially valuable for group study. Discusses twelve parables and does an especially fine job of formulating questions and providing examples germane to their contemporary application.

Harrington, Wilfrid J. *A Key to the Parables,* Paulist Press, 1964.
   A brief, well-written study that relies heavily on Jeremias (see below) in trying to ascertain the meaning of the parables in their "first" setting, the ministry of Jesus. Only the parables in Luke's Gospel are discussed.

Hunter, A. M. *Interpreting the Parables,* SCM, second ed., 1964.
   A useful summary of the history of parables interpretation and of contemporary study. Lists and comments on some sixty stories and parabolic-type sayings.

Hunter, A. M. *The Parables Then and Now,* Westminster, 1971.
   A sequel to the author's previously mentioned book. In his first book he emphasized what the parables meant originally in the lifetime of Jesus. In this one he stresses more their message for today.

Jeremias, Joachim. *New Testament Theology,* Vol. One, *The Procla-mation of Jesus,* SCM, 1971.

A rich compendium of the author's many years of research into the life, times and teachings of the Jesus of history.

Jeremias, Joachim. *The Parables of Jesus,* SCM, rev. ed., 1963.

The most important single study of the parables in modern times. Indispensable for all advanced study. In this work (which has gone through many printings) Jeremias demonstrates the way the parables were shaped by their use in the early church and so clears the way for identifying the earliest texts and their meaning in the life of Jesus.

Jeremias, Joachim. *Rediscovering the Parables,* SCM, 1966.

An abridged paperback edition of the previously mentioned larger work, with its more technical sections removed. The aim and content remain the same: "to go back to the oldest form of the parables attainable and to try to recover what Jesus himself meant by them."

Keck, Leander. *A Future for the Historical Jesus,* Abingdon, 1971.

A pioneering work that begins to explore the theological consequences of modern Gospel research. Concludes with an essay on "Jesus, the Parable of God."

Kingsbury, J. D. *The Parables of Jesus in Matthew 13, A Study in Redaction-Criticism,* S.P.C.K., 1969.

The focus of this detailed study is not the parables as originally taught by Jesus, but the parables as they were interpreted and understood by Matthew. A very useful analysis of the way the early Christians began to use these stories for their own edification.

Ladd, George Eldon. *The Presence of the Future,* Eerdmans, 1974.

A comprehensive treatment of New Testament eschatology, with special attention to the parables. This is a revision of the author's older work, *Jesus and the Kingdom,* Harper & Row, 1964.

Linnemann, Eta. *Parables of Jesus,* S.P.C.K., 1966.
A very thorough introduction and exposition of twelve parables, focusing on their original meaning as "language events" in the life of Jesus.

Mitton, C. Leslie. *Jesus, the Fact Behind the Faith,* Eerdmans, 1974.
A simply written, generally conservative account of contemporary approaches to Gospel study, with a good chapter on "Criteria for Distinguishing Historical from Nonhistorical."

Perrin, Norman. *Jesus and the Language of the Kingdom,* Fortress Press, 1976.
Although ranging wider than the parables, this book contains a very useful history of the modern interpretation of the parables of Jesus, together with a fresh attempt to relate these to the central theme of Jesus' teaching, the kingdom of God.

Perrin, Norman. *Rediscovering the Teaching of Jesus,* Harper & Row, 1967.
A sometimes technical, sometimes skeptical work that nevertheless is full of stimulating insights into many facets of the contemporary quest of the historical Jesus.

Rhoads, David M. *Israel in Revolution: 6-74 C.E., A Political History Based on the Writings of Josephus,* Fortress Press, 1976.
Another excellent source for reconstructing an accurate picture of the social and political milieu of Jesus' parabolic teachings.

Rivkin, Ellis. *A Hidden Revolution, The Pharisees Search for the Kingdom Within,* Abingdon, 1978.
A sympathetic study of Pharisaism by a leading Jewish scholar. Important for a background understanding of the group with whom Jesus in his parables was more intensely engaged than any other.

Summers, Ray. *The Secret Sayings of the Living Jesus,* Word Books, 1968.

A simply written account and discussion of the Gospel according to Thomas, together with a translation arranged in parallel columns with the comparable passages in Matthew, Mark, Luke and John. An excellent introduction to this remarkable new Gospel discovery.

TeSelle, Sallie. *Speaking in Parables, A Study in Metaphor and Theology,* Fortress Press, 1975.
    This is not so much a study of Jesus' parables as an explanation of the stimulation that this way of "doing theology" might have, if taken seriously by contemporary theology.

Throckmorton, Burton Jr., ed. *Gospel Parallels, A Synopsis of the First Three Gospels,* Thomas Nelson, third ed. rev., 1967.
    An indispensable tool for the study of the synoptic Gospels. Parallel texts are arranged in parallel columns for easy comparison.

Tolbert, Mary Ann. *Perspectives on the Parables, An Approach to Multiple Interpretations,* Fortress Press, 1979.
    A sustained argument for the right of contemporary scholars to utilize the parables with the same freedom that the early church did. To counteract the anarchy that might arise from such an approach, the author calls for fidelity to the literary structure and surface meanings of these stories.

Via, Dan Jr. *The Parables,* Fortress Press, 1967.
    A pioneering study of the literary qualities of the longer parables, with a unique classification of them into "tragic" and "comic."